HOPE

IN 24

HOURS

HOPE
IN 24
HOURS

Your Situation Can Change for the Better

By: Comedian Nazareth
Foreword by: Chonda Pierce

Editor: Alissa Griffith
Comedy Editor: Robert G. Lee

Comedy Crusade
1163 Merlin Lane
Corona, CA 92881

Published 2018 by Comedy Crusade
Printed at Thomson-Shore Inc., Dexter MI

20 19 18   1 2 3 4

ISBN: 978-0-9894375-1-6
Library of Congress Control Number: 2018903061

Dedication

I dedicate this book to the love of my life, my best friend for over 20 years, my wife, Maha. They say, "behind every great man there is a great woman," but in my case, it should say, "beside every great woman there is an average man taking all the credit."

If it weren't for my wife, I never could have impacted the lives God allowed me to impact or be able to tour with all the peace of mind knowing that my home is in order.

Thank you, Baby. The proceeds from this book should go to your favorite Department store!

FOREWORD

There is phrase that I have heard often in my life. "Timing is everything!"

In comedy — timing is imperative. You can have great material. Funny words placed in the right place, the punchline settled at the end — but, rush through the delivery and you will lose the impact and more importantly — no one will laugh. And no one laughing for a comic can be horrifying! I know, because I'm a Comedian! That panicked feeling when the sweat drips down your back as the audience seems to be drift further and further away. It can be downright painful.

My friend, Nazareth is a Comedian too. We have been friends for over a decade. His timing is impeccable. I have envied his brilliant material and watched him grab an audience back within seconds if something didn't go like he wanted. I have learned so much by watching his tap dance with the audience.

More importantly, I have learned the greatest lesson about timing by watching his life. The valuable lessons in this book will demonstrate the powerful timing that God has for every life. Learning that you cannot rush things and how to wait on the Lord is, well . . . it's timely. Nazareth has taught me to trust what God has—let His timing take over. And if there was ever a story about perfect timing—It is the life of Nazareth. Find a comfy chair, sit back and watch his story unfold. Because, timing really is everything.

Chonda Pierce
Comedian, Author, Recording Artist

ENDORSEMENTS

"I've known Nazareth for over 20 years as a Comedian who brings laughter and encouragement to people. Hope in 24 Hours is no exception This book will encourage you and give you hope."

—**Josh McDowell**

"Comedian Nazareth is both funny and profound in *Hope in 24 Hours*. He makes you laugh, but more important he authentically points you to the God of Hope who transforms lives and fills us with His hope."

—**Jud Wilhite, Senior Pastor, Central Church; author, Pursued**

"Nazareth has experienced more than once how God can change your entire life in 24 hours. He has faced challenges and found how God brings the victory. He has listened to God and found God's promises are real. He has followed God and found his life is better now than he could ever have imagined. I have seen this up close and I have loved that through it all Nazareth has laughed and caused all of us to laugh with him. This book and this man will show you how the "Joy of the Lord is your strength" (Nehemiah 8:10).

—Chuck Booher—Nazareth's Pastor!
Crossroads Christian Church, Corona, CA

"Nazareth has an infectious sense of humor and an infectious sense of hope. In fact, his unique gift to make us laugh is what God uses to open the door of our hearts so that we can be invaded with the hope that only comes from above. Get ready to be infected by hope."

—Gene Appel, Senior Pastor—Eastside
Christian Church, Anaheim, CA

" My good friend Nazareth has a vibrant relationship with God, seeks to live a life of purity, and loves his family in the way that is a model for us all. What happened to Nazareth, can happen to you. He found a Life Saver and Life Changer in Jesus Christ, and in this book, he shares the miraculous ways that God changed his life. May this book inspire and encourage you, if you're looking for what you cannot find, or if you're looking for a source of encouragement in your own life. I hope you will read it, and then pass it on to another person who is looking for what you were looking for. "

—Pastor Bob Grenier,
Senior Pastor—Calvary Chapel Visalia

W A R N I N G

Don't let this book fool you. It reads like a memoir but be careful, as you are reading it, you will be encouraged, inspired, and filled with hope and patriotism.

You will be encouraged to look at your challenges that are similar to what Nazareth went through, and expect and pray, for similar results. You will be encouraged to know that your situation can change, for the better, in 24 hours or less.

- ⏲ If your challenge is finances, read chapter 12. (Banking on God)

- ⏲ If your challenge is relationships and finding a spouse, read chapter 6.

- ⏲ If your challenge is your children, read chapter 8.

◔ If you challenge is Spiritual, read chapter 4.

◔ If you are stuck in your job and wanting to do what you love to do, read chapter 7. If you are hoping to restore a relationship with a loved one, read chapter 16.

But we highly recommend reading the entire book since it reads as a memoir.

You will also notice the transformation that happened to Nazareth as you are going from chapter one to the end of the book. That transformation is available to you as well.

INTRODUCTION

MY GOAL IN WRITING THIS BOOK IS TWO-FOLD; first to show you, through stories and events from my life, that God's plans for us are different than our plans. Often, tomorrow can bring a whole new solution that we didn't even expect or think about.

Your problem can be solved, your situation can change, your financial debt can be removed, your fears can be eliminated. It may sound too good to be true, but all that can happen in 24 hours or less. Really!

I will share stories with you from my life—about how God took my guilt and fear away in 24 hours; how He answered my prayer and gave me a wife in 24 hours; how He changed my financial situation in 24 hours.

Give God a day and He can change your life. Give him a week and He can make a whole new world!

I will also share the story of my life with you. Had I lived in any other part of the world it would be dramatically different and mundane.

That's the second goal from writing this book; to give you an appreciation for our country; the United States of America. (When I refer to the United States of America in this book, I refer to it as America. I don't mean North America, but America. That's what we called it when I lived in Kuwait.)

I hope by the end of this book that you become more optimistic about your situation and less fearful of the problems you are facing. Also, unless I'm way off target (or you're a terrorist), you will be thankful for living in this country.

I would love for the whole world to read this book, including my wife and children. Because of that, I will refrain from sharing some of the stories from my life where the details are a little too lurid, or immoral, or just too flat out embarrassing to share.

If I put them down in print I'm afraid my kids would never let it go. They already tell me I don't know what I'm doing. No matter what they think, I'm no fool. I'm not going to give them ammunition!

Just know that before I turned my life over to God, I hit rock bottom. Maybe one day, if we meet at an airport or at one of my concerts, I will share with you some of those stories that I can't share in this book (for a small fee of course—your understanding).

One of the stories I can tell started on a typically hot summer day in Southern California. I was fighting traffic in my red, sports Nissan 200, going North on the 405 Freeway heading towards 3rd Street and La Brea, in Los Angles to pick up my manager, Chuck Harris.

Chuck was a very smart Jewish manger, in his late 50s.

Golden-white hair, large distinguished glasses; perpetually dressed in a black suit. Chuck always reminded me that I was his favorite Palestinian. I don't think he knew any other Palestinians. Chuck took a chance on me and it was starting to pay off. No manager would sign a Comedian that early in their career, but he saw potential in me.

Chuck lived in a two-story home, in a nice Jewish Neighborhood in Los Angeles. The house was crowded with art collections and several juke boxes that he collected. Chuck was always on the phone making deals. He only represented two Comedians; Brad Stine and me.

I picked up Chuck and we drove to the NBC studios lot to watch one of his clients perform on the Jay Leno show. There, I got to meet Jay Leno for the first time. I met him twice after that. Once at the Comedy & Magic Club in Hermosa Beach and another time with our mutual friend, Jimmy Brogan.

We watched the show from the Green Room. That same room where all the stars that appeared on the Tonight's show with Johnny Carson and later Jay Leno hung out in before getting on stage. I stood in that room quietly, dreaming of the day I could possibly be a guest on the Tonight Show.

I was very proud of how fast I was climbing the ladder to fame. That night Chuck told me he, and his assistant Richard, were working on a pilot to pitch to NBC called: "Fish Out of Water—A Middle Eastern Man in America."

At that time, I was the only Middle Eastern Comedian I knew of working the clubs. A few years after I left Hollywood, some Arab comics started appearing on the scene.

Comedians like Ahmed Ahmed, Maysoon Zayid and various others (in my opinion, the two mentioned above are very funny).

I told Chuck not to tease me. He said, "No. I can and will

make it happen." He knew the right writers and the right executives at NBC.

Ever since I was a child, I have loved to make people laugh, loved the attention, loved the applause. I always wanted to become a performer, but living in Kuwait, as a child, I didn't know how that could ever happen!

Through fate or good fortune, things were looking good for me. I'm not trying to brag, but I was getting standing ovations and huge laughter every time I went on stage. I was doing the comedy circuit and was booked to do a week in Las Vegas at the Aladdin Comedy Club.

I'm glad I wasn't wearing hats or turbans as my head was getting bigger and bigger. Fans were buying me drinks at clubs. Since I was building a name in Hollywood, I became more attractive to female fans. That's one of those unspoken perks that draws average looking guys like me to Hollywood; namely, success can get you just as many girls as money can. And if you have both, well, forget about it!

I never worried where to hang out after any show since there were always fans offering free drugs and free other things (Kid Alert: the drugs were non-prescription and the "free other things" were items like chips and salsa.)

Hollywood had something to offer me; Fame, Wealth and a Fun Life Style. Americans love celebrities and the way my career was going, I was heading there and heading there fast.

Then one day, everything changed in 24 hours . . . .

CHAPTER 1

HOLY LAND TO HOLY TOLEDO

I was born in the Holy Land to a father who was a Jeweler and a mother who decided to become a French Teacher. At one point she decided to become a nun, but later changed her mind and married my dad. I'm glad she did. It would've been difficult for her to have me being a nun. Another virgin from that land? Been there done that.

My parents lived in the Gaza Strip, a city in the Southern part of Israel. Currently it is run by the Islamic Group Hamas; not the friendliest people on the planet.

My mom was born in Jaffa, near Jerusalem. At age 12, she and her family fled as refugees in 1948 to Gaza. That really affected my mom in every aspect, especially in the way she raised us.

As a result of how difficult her childhood was, my mother was very protective of us. She didn't want us to leave the house if we didn't have to. I always thought this was a great reason to skip school, but somehow going to school was on her list of "must do's."

I love my mother but at that time she was fearful, controlling, and pessimistic—on her good days! Despite her own baggage, she loved us. She would do anything for us.

Many women from her generation who became refugees had the same personality.

I was the youngest of three brothers. My last name is Rizkallah (which I now pronounce as "Smith" for immigration purposes). It means "God's blessing" in Arabic.

In my family, God's blessing was just something we said but didn't put a lot of stock in.

God's son Jesus was a famous guy from history whose house we went to on big holidays.

Like my ancestors for generations before, my parents were born into an ancient Christian denomination called Greek Orthodox.

Neither mom nor dad liked Mass, so my family only attended services when they figured they were supposed to. "I went to church on Christmas and Easter, but it all sounded Greek to me."

If you're following along, that makes me a Christian Middle Easterner. People in the West don't think we exist. Most Westerners think everyone who lives in the Holy Land are either Jewish or Muslim. To be blunt about it, the Christians from my home town are the ones that maintained Christianity until we handed it to the West.

We're the original Christians. It's called The Holy Land for good reason. Most of Jesus' followers started in that area. Not every disciple or apostle went to Europe. Some stayed, while others went to Lebanon, Syria, Egypt, or Iraq.

I get asked a lot: Are you Jewish, or are you Muslim? People are amazed when I tell them I'm a Christian. They ask, "When did you convert?" I tell them, "My grandpa did at 33 AD."

It was hard for Christians during the Islamic Invasions and the Ottoman rule, where you either had to become a Muslim, pay taxes or be killed by the sword. You could either lose your religious freedom, your money or your life. What a choice!

To protect their congregations, some priests in the Holy Land sold the gold icons that decorated the inside of their churches to pay for the high taxes demanded by the Ottomans, the ruling Islamic power of that time.

My great grandfather decided to pay high taxes to remain a Christian. There was no refund at the end of his tax year. No deductions. In that area of the world, if you're still a Christian, it means that your great grandfather had to pay a lot of money for it. It's like paying a large membership fee to go to church. In other words, Christians at that time were persecuted but united...and mostly broke. When you get that kind of treatment, you don't care if you're Lutheran, Baptist, Catholic, or Coptic; you're a Christian.

Can you imagine paying $50,000 a year just to go to church? Makes Sunday morning decisions a lot easier. If you paid that much money just to belong, skipping a service or sleeping in would feel like you're throwing your money away.

If everyone paid $50,000 a year just to belong, our churches would be rolling in it! Most would probably have Valet parking, real wine for communion, special request worship songs, and a heated Baptismal pool. And if the Pastor didn't give a moving powerful message every single weekend, he'd be in charge of the Valet parking by the next.

In 1965 my father moved to Kuwait to seek work. The area was getting ready for the 1967 War and many refugees moved from all over the Holy land to Gaza. Gaza was crowded back then but it is much more crowded today.

Kuwait is a rich country because of the Oil. I capitalize the word "Oil" because where I'm from, it is considered Holy. If you're geographically challenged, Kuwait is located in Western Asia, at the tip of the Persian Gulf (If you live in Kuwait, you call it the Arabian Gulf). It shares borders with Iraq and Saudi Arabia.

Oil was discovered in Kuwait and many families from all over the middle East moved there to seek employment in that desert area.

In 1966 Mom put her three boys, aged 6, 5, and 3, all dressed in white fur jackets, in a small, black and white Taxi and we drove six hours through the Saini desert from Gaza to Cairo, Egypt. I can't begin to imagine what the Taxi's Driver's tip was.

We spent the night at a hotel there. All I remember was that Nassir, the president of Egypt at the time, was having a parade and we were able to watch it from the hotel balcony. Not a single floating camel or pyramid float in the whole parade!

The next morning, we flew to Kuwait. It was my first time on a plane. Then it was the thrill of a lifetime. Now I'd pay anything to never step on another one.

Dad met us at the airport and we started our life in a Country where we knew we were 2nd class citizens. We could never become citizens regardless of how long we lived there. We couldn't own a home or buy a business. You pray that you never get in trouble with a Kuwaiti citizen because the law is always on their side . . . . regardless.

I started attending school when I was 5. In Kuwait, you go to Elementary school for four years, then Middle school for four years and then High school for four years. I attended Elementary and High school at the same private all boy school. Both of my older brothers attended there as well.

When I was little, around three or four, when our relatives visited us at our apartment, Mom would stay in the kitchen and would ask me to go out in the living room and entertain them by telling them jokes. She would bribe me by giving me money to tell jokes. I think you can guess where this is going.

From the very beginning, I have loved to make people laugh. At family gatherings back then, I was never out playing with the other kids, I was entertaining the adults. For a four-year-old, it was an impressive career. I got an agent. He was the five-year-old next door. He got me a gig performing at his house. He demanded twenty percent. I refused.

He sued. We parted ways.

In school I was an "A" student and always helped the lazy students do well in their exams. That made me popular. I wasn't good at sports but liked to ditch school to smoke and go to the Girl's School in the vicinity.

It's different now, but when I was growing up Principals and Teachers were allowed to slap students. Not only that, they were allowed to hit us with sticks and insult us.

Remember that old kid's song, "Sticks and stones can hurt my bones, but words can never harm me?" In our school we got both! And believe me, they both hurt.

I remember getting caught during school with my lazy student friends, and we would get sent to the Principal's office. I would watch them all get slapped on the face or hit by a stick on their behinds, but not me. The Principal always looked at me and said, "You're an "A" student. Don't hang out with these losers. Go back to your class."

During my teen years, we attended an elite private club where most of the Westerners in Kuwait spent their weekends. The British Nationals, the Italians and the Americans were all regulars. A few Kuwaiti families were members as well. Although Kuwait was a dry country, people were able to drink alcohol inside that club. Girls wore bikinis and boys were allowed to be alone with girls in that club. You could get arrested for doing any one of those activities outside of the club. It was called The Gazelle Club. We called it Paradise.

I thrived in that club. I had great friends. I would water ski, play billiards, tennis, volleyball and bowling.

I was never short of money. My dad made a good living. He spent everything he made on us. We bought expensive clothes. I owned 4 or 5 Italian suits before I turned 17. I didn't have a backpack; I carried a leather brief case to school, with a gold cross pen. One time, one of the teachers told me that his one-month salary wouldn't pay for one of these pens. I gave it to him. I didn't know the value of money back then.

Looking back, it never occurred to me that I might be a little spoiled. I just got whatever I asked for. My dad never taught us how hard it is to make money. He worked night and day to provide for us and we took it for granted. My mom enjoyed that life style. They didn't think of saving any money.

When my dad left Kuwait to come to the US. He didn't have a penny to his name. He had us. I came to appreciate him for the life he offered me, and I was soon willing to spend every penny I made on him. In a strange way, my brothers and I were his 401-K plan. He diversified. He had 3 boys. We proved to be, by the end of his life, the best retirement plan he had.

In the Middle East, at that time, parents subliminally instilled in their children's mind that they are obligated to take care of them when they get old. There was no such thing as a Retirement Home or Senior Living. You take care of your parents until they die and then some.

Americans think logically. Arabs think emotionally. After living in the US for over 30 years, it does make sense to have your elderly parents in a Retirement Community. Why not spend your sunset years with other people your own age under the watchful eye of a trained medical staff?

That was considered shameful for us to do in the Middle East. If Middle Eastern mothers have a specialized skill, it's raising their children with guilt . . . to feel guilty about not offering the best treatment to their mothers.

I remember one time a cousin of ours decided to move his mom to a home. When my mom caught wind of it, she made sure I knew how bad that cousin was, to do such a shameful thing. I said, "Mom, don't worry. I will never put you in a home, but it does makes sense." She didn't speak to me for a month.

In 1979, back before we moved from Kuwait, my oldest brother, Ramzi, graduated from High School. He was accepted at a University in Glasgow, Scotland. Dad decided to take all three boys and mom to Spain and then over to England to enjoy one last trip together as a family. That was a memorable vacation. It was my first time leaving Kuwait since I arrived there when I was three. I was excited to be in the West for the first time in my life.

We spent a week in Spain. During our visit, my brother and I, along with a friend of ours, attended a bullfight. We used to watch bullfights on TV but being there in the arena was different.

It was not fair for the bull. Several bullfighters came out and spent almost an hour tiring the bull. And when the bull was on his last breath, the Celebrity Bullfighter came out to finish the bull up.

And people cheered for the bullfighter! Not me. I cheered for the bull. During one round, a large angry bull charged and hit one of the fighters. He sent him flying up in the air and then down. Two clowns came out to distract the bull. I jumped off my seat cheering for the bull. It was so quiet in the arena, you could hear a bullfighter drop. The entire arena stared at me with angry looks. I'm glad I didn't speak Spanish since I knew for sure, from the look on people's faces, they were not praising me for my choice.

I have always cheered for the underdog. That's what I love about America. Americans love the underdog. For some reason we never ask why the upper dog was allowed to get on top in the first place. That's not important. All we care about is rooting for the dog underneath to get up and put that mean ole' top dog in his place!

But now that I think about it, other than sporting events, I can't come up with another area where we like the underdog. In health care, I don't want my surgeon to be the underdog. The one whose only residency available was a Vet Hospital. No, if someone's going to cut me open, I want the top dog!

Anyway, we left Spain and spent another week in England. We visited the city of Cambridge where the famous Cambridge University is located. It was gorgeous and loaded with history, but I had no desire to attend a college in Great Britain. I always wanted to go to school in America.

That vacation was the last time our entire family was together.

The five of us weren't under one roof until Ramzi came to visit us in Newport Beach, CA, where we lived at the time, almost 20 years later.

Ramzi was the typical type "A" personality; always in a hurry and short fused. He also looked more like our mom than dad. My brother Emad, and I, look more like our dad. I'm not saying who won or who lost, just stating facts.

My brother Emad, who was a year younger than Ramzi, and two years older than me, followed him the next year. I was alone at home for the next few years. No siblings, just me preventing my parents from having an empty nest.

I left Kuwait 6 years before the invasion of Iraq in the early 90's.

I was accepted at the University of Toledo, Ohio. I still remember the day I left for the airport. My Greek friend, Alex, came and picked me up to take me to the airport. I saw my dad crying, for the second time in his life, when he said goodbye to me. The first time dad cried, is when he heard of the death of his younger brother, Shafik. His brother was 41 years old and died of a massive heart attack. He lived in Jordan at the time. Dad had 5 brothers and 3 sisters, four of whom lived inKuwait.

Then Dad's older brother died at 51 from a heart attack. He lived in the Gaza Strip at the time. I don't know if the heart thing is hereditary, but believe me, I stay in shape just in case!

I was the last bird to leave the nest. It wasn't a nest, it was a tent. I'm just kidding. We lived in a large flat in a decent part of Kuwait.

When I left Kuwait, I left for good and never came back. One day I might go visit. I did have some nice Kuwaiti friends. To live in a country where you feel that you are not treated equally really bothered me.

God bless America. If you were born in America or have lived here for a while, you can become a citizen. You can own a home. You can own your own business. You can vote. How wonderful is that! I'm sure you can understand that after what I've come from, I will never take that for granted.

So, there I was, on a plane flying thousands of miles to my new home. First stop, of all places, Toledo, Ohio.

Even then I knew my life was about to change......

CHAPTER 2

NAZARETH THE BUCKEYE

JFK

Leaving Kuwait, I flew Kuwait Airways in a smoke-filled airplane. I was so nervous I think contributed most of the smoke since I was basically a chain smoker on that flight. I don't know how the pilot saw out the window because the smoke was so heavy in my section, I couldn't see the Stewardess.

Four and a half packs later, I arrived at London Heathrow airport in transit to John F. Kennedy Airport in New York. I can only vaguely remember the flight from Kuwait to London. My mind was on the friends and family I left behind, not to mention the memories and good times I had there.

Unbelievably, my dream was becoming a reality; to come to America. Ever since I was 10 years old, I had dreamed of coming to America. My 4th grade friend at school, Wael, migrated with his family to the fabled land of New Jersey. He filled my head with stories about it before he left. From that day on, I wanted to go to America. And now, I was actually going there! I was hours away from landing on the greatest place on Earth. I kept telling the woman seated next to me to pinch me. I thought I was dreaming. She thought I was some kind of pervert.

I'm sorry to say that even with all the social media available today, I cannot find my old friend, Wael. Maybe he changed his name. Maybe he's boycotting Facebook.

Regardless, he's lost to me. Sometimes I wonder what it would be like to have a High School reunion. For most immigrants and for Military brats, the reality is that you never go back to where you went to school, to the old friends. I'm not complaining. I live in America now. Besides, I heard someone blew up my old High School.

It is hard to find old friends since most immigrants shorten their name when they come to America, to make it easier for Americans to pronounce it. Mohammed, becomes Mo, Jaffar becomes Jeff, and Fatima becomes Fay. That could be dangerous. Can you imagine changing your name from Abdulla to Sam? Now imagine you are crossing the street and a Mack truck is barreling towards you and you don't see it. Your friends scream, "Sam watch out! Sam watch out!" But your brain is thinking, "I'm Abdulla." By the time you figure out that you're Sam you're nothing but a spot on the pavement.

I sometimes wondered why Americans don't make their names longer when they come to the Middle East. For example,

Bob can be called Kabob, Barbara will be Baklava, and Phil can become Fala-Phil.

After flying for thousands of miles, when I heard the captain announce, "We are about to land at John F. Kennedy Airport," it was a sobering moment for me. I was going to be in a land where I didn't know anyone. I didn't know what was awaiting me in America. I had a friend from school who lived in Brooklyn, New York. I had his number but that's about it. I was arriving in a new Country where I barely spoke the language. I only knew the America that I'd seen in movies.

I didn't know what to expect. Did America look like Gotham City in Batman, the prairie in Little House on the Prairie and the Walton's, or like John Wayne's America?

I got off the plane and walked towards the Immigration Officers. They looked at my student visa, stamped it and the officer said, "Welcome to America." Oh, how sweet the sound.

Welcome to America: the land of opportunities. Where everything was either legal or accessible. I was no longer under the tight control of my mother. I could drink, stay up late or experiment with drugs. Finally, I could be cool. (Note to my kids: I was wrong.

Drugs do not make you cool. Drugs make your hair and teeth fall out. I was young and stupid. Like you are now. Do not listen to my teenage self. Listen to the much older and wiser, dad-"self".)

Many years later, while I was walking on the boardwalk in Huntington Beach, CA, I ran into an old Egyptian man walking with a cane. He said hello. I stopped and talked with him for a while. He gave me the best advice anyone could give. He said, "Son, you are still young. What's so great about America is that you can do anything you want. If you choose to live an immoral and destructive life, you can excel, and you will find the people who will help you live like that. But if you choose to live a moral life, you can excel at that as well and you will find the people who will as well."

That really is a great description of America. When I lived in Kuwait, I was warned so many times by well-meaning and mostly religious Muslims that Americans were immoral people. Their women were loose, their men were alcoholics and substance abusers, their families were broken, and they had no morals. At that time my first thought was, "Sign me up!" But after living in this country for over 30 years, I must say, I've met the most moral, conservative, and God-fearing people here in America. I've met families in Texas where their teenagers dressed modestly, and they called me "Sir". My own kids won't call me "Sir". Makes me want to move to Texas.

In the Arabic and Islamic culture, people hid their sins; they didn't talk about it. They covered them up. They didn't talk about their problems, they hid them. They also hid their children that were mentally or sometimes physically handicapped. It is a shame issue. They didn't want the neighbors to know they had imperfect children. Well, all the neighbors knew, but the family continued to hide their imperfect children.

That's what I love about America. They treat special-needs people with dignity and respect. They give them the best services offered. They make special laws to protect them and make their life as normal as it could be. I joke about that when I say that in parts of the Middle East, hospitals are not handicap-friendly! In America, even drug houses have wheelchair ramps!

If you live in the Middle East and you're reading this, I want you to know that in America, you can find the Godliest people;

God fearing people who want nothing more than to raise their families in the fear of the Lord. They don't drink and do drugs. Their daughters are virgins until marriage and they love to serve. The myth is shattered.

Back to JFK. I walked out into the busy baggage claim area. I had to get my luggage, find a hotel for the night, and then fly out the next day to Ohio where I would supposedly spend the next four years at the University of Toledo.

I found my luggage. As I was turning around, a man in his 30's approached me and said, "Are you looking for a Cab?" I replied, "Cab? What's a Cab?" He said, "A taxi." I said "Yes." He said, "Where are you heading?" I told him I wanted to find a hotel somewhere close to the airport.

He carried my luggage and took me to his car. I don't remember if it was a taxi car or not, but I knew there was no meter. I didn't know taxis had to have meters. He drove me for about 10 minutes and stopped at a hotel. He got out of the car and got my luggage out. I asked him how much I owed him? He opened a little book, looked at it and said, "$187.00." I was shocked. America is expensive! If that's what it costs to take a cab ride for 10 minutes, somehow, I didn't think the money I had with me was going to last until my senior year. If everything in America was that expensive, I wasn't sure I could make it to the next weekend.

I gave him a $13 tip. My first $200 expense. I walked to the hotel counter, and my first question was: "How much does it cost for a taxi ride from the Airport to your hotel?"

The receptionist replied: "Not more than $15." I told her, "I just paid $200." She said, "Oh honey, I'm sorry. There are con-artists like that who cheat and take advantage of tourists. I'm sorry."

I said, "That's OK. I'm sure there will be more."

But honestly, that $200 lesson taught me not to be taken advantage of. I made sure it would never happen again, and it didn't. So, all things considered, it was a cheap lesson.

The next morning, my friend Marwan, my only friend from NY, came to the hotel. He spent few hours with me and drove me to the airport to fly out to Toledo. He jokingly asked for $187 for his fare. I paid him, but he got no tip!

Toledo

Toledo, believe it or not, was the party town for me. I arrived at the international student office. The lady at the desk asked me where I was staying. I informed her that I had signed up and paid a deposit to stay at the University dorms. But honestly, I didn't feel like staying at the dorms. They sounded like they'd be too confining.

College for me was my escape from Alcatraz. I grew up with a mother who loved me but always said "No" to everything. No, you can't stay out late. No, you can't sleep over at your friend's homes. No, you can't invite friends to come over. Also, Kuwait was a dry country. So that's no to alcohol. No to beer. Therefore, coming to college meant freedom from mom, freedom from the Islamic culture, freedom from the Arabic culture. I wanted to be free. And in Toledo, I was free indeed. Or so I thought.

I was like a kid in a candy store.

I asked the Student Adviser at the International Student Office if there were other options other than the dorms. A student behind me jumped in and said, "Yes, there are." His name was Basaam, and he was from Jordan. He told me that he's been on the waiting list to get into the dorms, but nothing was available. On the spot, he said he'd gladly exchange with me. He lived with 3 other students, in a two-bedroom house, on Bancroft Road near the school.

I was willing to trade. The Student Councelor had no problem with that either. We made the trade and I took a taxi (with a meter and everything!) to the hotel. While the taxi waited, I picked up my luggage and went to my first home outside of my family home.

The University was big. It may not seem big to you, but compared to where I grew up, it was huge! I adjusted quickly and loved the people. That's just who I am. I love people. I love to meet new people and I love to know people's stories. That made it easy for me to surround myself with friends.

My first friend in Toledo was Afif. He was my first roommate. He was originally from Southern Lebanon. A nice Christian, young man who loved to help. He had a pickup truck and took me around to do the grocery shopping and to enjoy the night life of Toledo. A few months later, Afif moved in with his girlfriend and I ended up moving to an apartment with a friend I knew from Kuwait. I stayed in touch with Afif until I left Ohio.

Our apartment manager had two jobs. One was to manage the apartments. The other was to deal drugs. That was my first introduction to marijuana. I quickly learned that weed and homework didn't work well together.

Toledo had an Engineering School and was full of students from the Middle East. While it would have been easy to stay with what was familiar, I wanted to hang out with my American friends since I wanted to learn the American culture and the language. I came to America to become an American. I kept the best the Middle Eastern Culture offered and added the best the American Culture offered. I'm a well cultured mutt.

The Bait Shop

While attending college in Toledo, I learned that my dad lost his job in Kuwait. That was not good news. That meant he had to leave Kuwait, since he was not a native Kuwaiti. His work visa was controlled by his employer. Every employer had full control over their employees. You could hate your job in Kuwait, but you couldn't tell your boss to take the job and shove it. Well, you could if you want to be deported.

In Kuwait, the stability of your family is dependent on your employer. He has your passport and he can fire you anytime. Once fired, you must leave the country in few weeks unless you find another job and get sponsored by that employer.

I told my mom, that dad could come and live with me. At that time, I started working at different odd jobs. A friend of mine owned a building right on Lake Erie. It was a large, one-story, white brick building on two acres of land, on the main street, Lakeshore Drive on Lake Erie. The fourth largest lake of the Great Lakes in North America.

My friend and I agreed to use the building to sell bait and tackle in the Summer. I didn't know the first thing about fishing or tackle. I thought tackle meant you ram into someone.

But I was determined to learn. I started spending my free time looking for old fishermen on the different docks around Lake Erie. They spent hours fishing quietly. I would go and sit next to them and start up a conversation. It helped me learn more American slang as well as learn about fishing. I asked hundreds of questions such as: What do you catch here? What kind of lure do you use? What kind of bait, rod, reel, and why?

Not one fisherman was bothered by my curiosity. They talked and talked and answered all my questions and then some. That winter, the boy from Kuwait who'd never caught a fish in his life became an expert on lake fishing.

I ordered the lures, reels, sinks, knives, line and everything a fisherman needed to fish on the lake.

During the winter, all the bait and tackle shops are closed. They open beginning in April and close at the end of September. I was ready for the season. My friend's dad, Al, was a bait dealer. He provided me with the minnows. Another dealer sold me Night Crawlers. (That's worms for you foreigners.) Yes. Slimy worms. I bought them by the tray and then I had to count 12 worms at a time and put them in a small Styrofoam cup with some dirt and sell them by the dozen. It was disgusting!

Customers started stopping by the store. We kept the name, Alvin Bait Store. People called me Alvin. I didn't mind. It was difficult to say Nazareth for them. Fishermen were nice people. I never felt I didn't belong around them. They bought the minnows and went on Charter boats to go fishing for Walleye. The best fish ever. Sometimes they invited me to go fishing with them.

I worked from 7 AM until 9 PM every day, seven days a week, during Summer. I never complained. I loved it. I lived in a tiny room behind the store, with one small room that I furnished with a sofa bed and a recliner. It had a little bathroom with a shower and a kitchenette. Luxury!

When fishermen came back, they always stopped by to show me their catch. Many times, they thanked me for choosing the right lure. It felt great to help people with something I didn't know anything about before. I took the time to learn, I was able to help. **God Bless America.** The dream is true; I can be anything I want to be. I'm a business owner.

In all my time at the bait shop, I never met a racist person. I never looked for them, I never anticipated or expected someone to be a racist. I'm not saying it does not exist. I'm not saying there are no racist people in this Country. There may be a few but most of America is not racist. I was never discriminated against.

A few months following the opening of the bait store, I was approached by a guy named Jeff. Jeff was a short guy and cocaine had done a job on his face. He was very skinny. He asked if I could hire him to clean fish for me. He wanted to use the back of my building to do fish cleaning. In return, he asked if he could park his small motor home on the side of the building on the property.

I agreed. I figured, if fishermen are coming back to show me their catch, we could offer to clean the fish for them—for a fee of course.

Jeff claimed to be the fastest fish cleaner in the United States using an electric knife. I bought a stainless-steel table, a sink and a large commercial fridge and we started the fish cleaning business. The sign said: *Fish Cleaning. No Bones About It.*

We even offered a money-back guarantee if you could find a bone. See, with an electric knife it is easy to cut the fish and slide against the skeleton without cutting into the bones. Then you simply flip the fish around and slide the knife between the skin and the meat and, bang, you end up with a fillet of fish! You do the same thing on the other side of the fish and you end up with two filets of fish in less than 10 seconds. That's right, 10 seconds! Jeff could clean 8 Walleyes in one minute!

Jeff was a great addition to the business, except, many times, I would have people waiting for him to come out to clean the fish and he would be passed out or over-dosed on drugs, in his little trailer where he lived with his pregnant wife. She kept apologizing for her husband's behavior.

I was forced to start cleaning fish. I watched Jeff enough to learn how to do it. At times when he was sober, we worked side by side. I got so good, I could clean 7 walleyes a minute. Not quite up to Jeff's record, but pretty good, considering I was just learning. That meant 15 walleyes a minute between the two of us. People would watch us as if it was a show. Some people didn't catch any fish but just came by to see me and Jeff clean them. Even then, show business was in my blood.

Sometime later, I met a guy named Lee. Lee had known Jeff from before and came to help us clean fish. Lee was a tough guy. A big guy... Like that old Jim Croce song said, you don't mess around with Lee. The guy had a temper. Surprisingly, Lee ended up becoming one of my best friends in Ohio. His son, Shea, his brother Kevin, and his late wife, Laurie, all became great friends. They would come to the store daily while Lee was helping me with the fish cleaning.

We ended up hiring a Contractor named Paul, and his brother to help us. These were a pair of tough guys. They drank beer and used cocaine. And they became my entourage.

After work, we would all go to the nearby tavern; Kelly's Bar, for a beer or two. They all called me "Boss". I was surrounded with five guys that were Construction Workers.

Tough guys. I remember one time, a rude guy from the bar tried to get smart with me, and before he knew it, four BIG All-American thugs, walked towards him. I believe that rude guy from the bar still holds the world's record for an apology.

People always wondered how I managed to keep these guys working for me. They showed up on time, stayed till the end of the work day and then even hung out with me. Somehow these guys felt like family hanging around the bait store. I was kind to them. I cared about them. Plus, I paid them in beer and cocaine. But I'm pretty sure they stuck with me because of my winning personality.

The fish house became the profitable part of the business. Later, Jeff left, and Lee and I were the main guys cleaning fish. I held the title, The Second Fastest Fish Cleaner in the United States with an Electric Knife. I challenged people to beat me. They couldn't. Only Jeff could do it and he worked for me.

I then opened another fish house in Marble head, Ohio. Business was booming. I was making money. My dad moved in with me. I drove to Detroit to pick him up. Dad was not the same guy. He looked defeated. I brought him back to where I lived. A place that smelled like fish. I was wearing Jeans, Tennis Shoes and a Wind Breaker. My dad had never seen me dressed like that.

When I lived in Kuwait, I wore the latest fashions; Leather Shoes, Italian Pants, the latest French or Italian suits. I probably owned only one pair of Designer Jeans. I hardly wore Jeans in Kuwait.

Dad came to Port Clinton in a suit and tie and wore Leather Shoes. A few weeks later he was wearing his first ever Tennis Shoes and Levi Jeans. I made him an American dad.

That year, we had a heavy winter in Port Clinton, Ohio. The wind chill factor was about 30 below. That was cold for me. I grew up in the desert of Kuwait. We never had snow growing up. Santa Claus had a bad time with his reindeers and sleighs. He got stuck in the sand. We didn't receive our gifts 'til mid-February.

For me to see snow was wonderful. What an experience. I loved it when it snowed in Ohio. Wow, everything was so white and clean. I loved it for about 2 days. Then it started to irritate me. I couldn't wear my regular shoes. I had to wear Long Johns. I hated those. They itch, and they make you look like a Ballet Dancer.

I hated having to shovel snow for free just to get my truck out of the driveway.

Since I had the bait store, I had to find bait for the fishermen for winter fishing. One way to get it was to go to frozen lakes, dig holes and catch minnows with our nets. Exciting. Not really. Not for the minnows. They thought," Wow, we're safe for the winter." Literally. No nets. No mass killing.

One day I was walking on a frozen pond towards the crew. My dad had just moved from Kuwait several days before. He was sitting in the truck watching us work in the freezing weather. His blood was not adjusted yet. He still didn't like the idea of a man wearing Long underwear. I wasn't about to convince him otherwise so, he preferred staying in the truck watching.

As I walked on the pond towards the busy crew, I felt like Jesus for few seconds. With my lack of experience, I stepped on some thin ice and within seconds, I was completely immersed in the ice-cold water. I went into shock. I couldn't pull myself out. I'm a great swimmer, but not in a frozen pond. I don't remember how long I was under, but it felt like Eternity (even though I haven't been to Eternity yet, and if I were I would still be there and will not have the chance to come back and tell you about it.) The only person who was watching me was dad. He jumped out of the truck and screamed to the crew, "My son! My son!"

Lee ran to the hole, stuck his arm in the freezing water and pulled me out with one hand. By then I looked like a Popsicle (blueberry/strawberry flavor). I had swallowed some water. I also had layers of frozen ice in-between my clothes. They took me back to the house, tore my clothes off, and wrapped me in blankets. I couldn't speak for the entire ride home. I mumbled words. Lee thought I was trying to say, "Thank you" Others thought I was saying "It is cold in here"; But what I was really trying to say to my friend and the rest of the crew that helped me was, "Hey don't waste your time. I didn't see any minnows under there."

Thank God for daddy watching.

A few months later, I drove with my dad to the Detroit Airport to pick up my mom. She was happy to see me and dad, but sad to leave Kuwait. Or, perhaps more accurately, she was sad to leave her standard of living. Mom was used to luxury that dad and his job offered, but life had changed.

The pendulum had swung and now I was the provider, and the decision maker for my parents. I knew my parents couldn't survive the cold in Ohio, so I started thinking seriously about moving South. We had an aunt that lived in Huntington Beach, California and we decided that was where we would move.

When the end of the fishing season came in September, I gave the business to my friend, bought a pickup truck and all three of us, my dad, mom and I started our 2300- mile drive to Southern California.

All we brought with us were our clothes. It was the first time in my life I had ever driven that far. Up to that point, I think I'd driven maybe a total of two hours at a stretch. This was going to take a bit more effort.

We drove all day and night until we got to Denver, Colorado. It was amazing to see mountains! We stopped at a hotel for the night, then we continued until we got to the golden state. We arrived at our destination at midnight. We didn't want to wake up my aunt, so we rested for a few hours in her driveway until morning.

I learned so many lessons in Ohio. I learned to appreciate America, Americans, and that you can be whoever you want to be. You can own a business, start another two businesses and nobody will stop you.

The sky is the limit here in America. Opportunities are all over the place. **God Bless America.**

If you're reading this, I want you to have hope to know that you can do anything you want to do in America if you are willing to work hard at it.

If I, as a student with an accent, can do it, you can too. Don't make excuses. . . . make plans!

In case you're wondering, in between working at my bait and tackle shop, drug dealing and fish filleting, I never managed to finish school. Even though I was not armed with a College Degree (I got that later, in California), and was saddled with two unemployed parents and clothes that permanently smelled of fish, I was ready to take on the world! I didn't have a clue what was waiting for me in California.

CHAPTER 3

CERTIFIED PUBLIC COMEDIAN

California

After we arrived on the Gold Coast, we spent a month with my aunt. She lived in a three-bedroom, two-story house on Magnolia and Pacific Coast Hwy., very close to the beach. My aunt had three kids—two boys and a girl. My mom and dad slept in one of the kid's rooms and I slept in the living room.

As a side note, one of the reasons I work so hard at my marriage is that I've already slept on the couch. I never need to go back there again.

During my month on the sofa, I visited several fishing places in Newport Beach and Balboa Peninsula. I spoke to several fishermen and bait store owners. I found out quickly that I knew nothing about ocean fishing. I knew I could learn it and excel at it, but I didn't have any seed money to invest in a new company, and I needed to make money quickly.

My mother kept pushing me to get a job with a paycheck. Any kind of day job. She did the same thing to my dad before. My dad was a Jeweler in the Gaza Strip. When he moved to Kuwait, his dream was to open his own Jewelry store. He planned to work a day job for a while and then work as a Jeweler. But my mom was fearful and encouraged him to stay at the day job.

I remember dad telling me on his death bed that his dream was to have his own Jewelry store and to be working as a Jeweler.

I applied to a new restaurant that just opened in Huntington Beach, called El Pollo Loco. Employees had to wear large Sombreros to work there. I applied but they never called me. Apparently, I wasn't Loco enough.

My first job in California was at a Temp Agency where they sent me to several companies to work for a day or two. I then got a second job, on the weekend, working for a baby furniture store in Laguna Hills called Marcy's Baby World. I was the Delivery guy. I figured that baby furniture is a lot lighter to carry than adult furniture. Later I got a job working for a Subway restaurant. After a few months, my temp job became permanent working for a large restaurant company. It was called Grace Restaurants; a fortune 500 company. It was later a leveraged buyout and they changed the name to Restaurant Enterprise Group.

I worked in the Payroll Tax Department. They first hired me as a temp employee to cover for a lady named Debbie who went on maternity leave. I sat in Debbie's cubical. Apparently, Debbie, who I never met, was a great employee. They loved her and told me that I couldn't change anything in her work space.

That was fine with me, except Debbie had pictures of her kids all over the cubical. She also had a huge 10x13 picture of her husband in red Speedos and it said:

I ♥ MIKE

Obviously, Mike was a European since, unless you're swimming in the Olympics, American guys don't wear Speedos.

I had to look at that picture every day. But worse than that, other employees who came to my cubical to ask for things, or to drop some paperwork, looked at the picture and made some inappropriate remarks to say the least. I spent the first two weeks working there explaining that this was not my cubical and that I was only here temporarily to cover for Debbie who was on a maternity leave.

After two weeks, I got tired of explaining and just played along. When asked how Mike was doing, I would say, "He's doing great. Thank you for asking!"

What was even worse is when pretty girls came to my cubical and looked at the picture, I knew that my chances of taking them on a date were ruined.

At one point I was working three jobs, seven days a week. For three years I didn't take a day off. Not a single weekend, not a vacation day nor a sick day. I needed the three jobs to pay for the house I rented for me and my parents, and to take care of the expenses. It was such a long, hard road that I'll admit there were a few times I actually wished I could just go back to sleeping on my aunt's couch!

I was the only one working and didn't believe in Food Stamps. I'm not saying there's anything wrong with using Food Stamps.

I think it is a great temporary relief when people are going through a hard time. But they weren't for me. **God Bless America** that these services are available to people who need it, but I promised myself that I would never be a burden on this Country. I came here to contribute.

Once I was hired as a permanent employee at Restaurant Enterprises Group, I was moved to an office with four ladies. It was wonderful to have my own space, but I missed Debbie's kids. And I still call Mike from time to time and ask him if I can borrow his red Speedo. He has no idea who I am.

Being in an office with four women, I'm sure you can guess I got an education! I learned how to gossip, what not to say to a woman, and, most importantly, what are the best kind of pantyhose. I never had sisters but those few years I spent in that office were a crash course on learning how to treat women.

The late eighties were the party years. I would leave work and if I didn't go to my night job, I would hang out with my friends from work. Lily was the party girl who planned the parties and the hangouts. She always brought along Andy, who, I came to discover, was a hitman.

Andy collected money from people who didn't pay at the "secret Home Casinos" near San Diego. This was before the Indian Casinos started popping up. Andy was a skinny guy, but you didn't want to mess with him. He was tough and carried guns.

In between the hard work and the parties, I joined a night school to learn how to use various computer programs like Basic. That's where I met Pammy Anne. Pamela was a beautiful person inside and out. She laughed at everything I said. She drove a monster truck and needed an elevator to get in the driver's seat. She was dating a bad guy. I kept telling her she could do better.

As it happens, we eventually lost touch. It wasn't until early 2017 when I found her again on Facebook. She has two kids and few grandkids. She left the bad boy and married a good man.

Lilly, Andy, and I used to go to parties on weekends after my weekend job and drink and use. At times, we would stay up until morning and wait for a bowling alley to open and then go hang out there. All along, my mom and dad would be home in that small house watching TV. When I got home, dad would take the car and go get groceries or take mom for a ride.

I then moved to the Payroll Department and befriended an Artist named Joe. He worked in the same department. Joe had long black hair. He looked like Steve Perry, the old lead singer for the band Journey. Joe was my height and drove an old black BMW.

One time on Halloween, back in those years, Joe and I decided to throw a party at his apartment in Santa Ana, CA. I was dressed like an Arab Sheik and Joe was a Pirate. Some people from our work showed up and many others who were not even invited. Thanks to a pimp named Captain, the drugs were flowing that night.

Our drug of choice was cocaine and Long Island Ice tea was the follow up drink. We were so high we didn't even keep track of time. The party lasted for 3 days with me, Joe, and few others being the common denominators. All we cared about is keeping people happy with enough booze.

At one point, we were so drunk we walked into 711 to buy some more beer. There was a tour bus parked there with its door open. Some of the tourists went down to buy stuff from the store. We started joking with the driver and found out he was going to Vegas so, we convinced him to take us to Vegas. He agreed.

At the last second, before leaving, we got sober enough to realize that we don't have more than $20 between us, we were dressed like an Arab Sheik and a Pirate and we were very drunk. The bus driver was kind enough to stop and let us out.

At that party, in order to get more drugs, I degraded myself and called Captain the pimp, "Sir." That's all I wanted from him. Drugs make you do stuff and deal with people you would've never ever talked to before.

Many years later, after turning my life to God, I met many guys like Captain, inside the hundreds of prisons I've visited, and I called them all "Sir". Not to get drugs, but as a sign of respect.

God used these experiences to teach me how to deal with inmates in prison and with drug addicts.

One-time, Joe and I went on a double date to a Mexican Restaurant. All the girl wanted to talk about was Jesus. I wasn't interested. Looking back, after I turned my life to God, I knew this was part of God's plan and she was part of God's army to recruit me into the Faith.

That night was memorable, because during dinner, the Mariachi band came to our table and offered to sing a song to the girls. With Joe's broken Spanish, we understood that it was $5 for 10 songs. So, we agreed to 10 songs. The Mariachi band spent half of the evening playing songs for our table. At the end, we handed them $5. They were so mad. It was $5 per song! Remember this was 1989 and $50 was more than we had to spend on dinner. It was an embarrassing night. It was the last time I had a Mariachi band sing for me.

Joe loved girls. All kind of girls. Short and tall, big and small, young and old. Sometimes I was impressed by his choice of girl-friends, other times I was disgusted. I, on the other hand, was more interested in the partying.

I'll never forget the day Joe and I had a day off from work and we hung out at the beach in Long Beach, CA. We both were sharing our dreams. His dream was to have his own Graphic Design Firm. Mine was to be a professional Comedian.

We were dreaming . . . not knowing that it would become a reality. A few years later, Joe decided to move to Texas. He got married and started his own firm. The last time I was in contact with him, he was doing very well. I lost touch with Joe for the next 20 years. One day, out of the blue, Joe called me and told me that he was living in a drug house. He lost his Firm, he got a divorce and remarried, and now has 3 children and is divorced from that one as well. He told me that he was moving to Myrtle Beach to be with his mother. From that point on, I've managed to stay in contact with him.

I found out that his children were living with his ex-wife and her girlfriend in Washington State. I was doing a show in Seattle and purchased a ticket for Joe to meet me in Seattle and spend time with his kids. It was great seeing him after such a long while.

Even though we had a great time catching up, he looked defeated. He was struggling with bi-polar and was cleaning up his life.

I was able to share with Joe what God has done in my life and we prayed together. We then realized we were at a Mexican restaurant and remembered the Mariachi band nightmare. As I walked out, I gave the band five dollars and told them I still owed them forty bucks.

I met Joe's kids briefly and then had to go to my show. Joe spent a few more days in Washington and went back to Myrtle beach only to move back to Dallas soon after.

One day, I received a call from Joe. He said that he and his current girlfriend, Emma, were staying at a motel and had no money whatsoever. They said they were hungry. I got the address of the motel, and, thanks to Google Earth, I was able to find the location. I then proceeded to find a nearby church. I found one close by. I called the church secretary. I introduced myself, talked about the Lord for few minutes and then told her about Joe and Emma. She prepared two large grocery bags from the church kitchen for them. I called Joe back and told him that there were two large grocery bags waiting for them across the street from the motel. To this day, Joe is amazed how I could do that. I told him, I'm in God's army. We have soldiers all over the world!

Thank you, Facebook

A few months later, I received a Facebook e-mail from Emma. She was wondering if I knew where Joe was. He left her, and she wanted to know if he was OK. I told Emma through the Facebook e-mail that what she needed, was not Joe. She needed Jesus. We communicated for few minutes, and I was able to share the Lord with her. I advised her to seek help. She then joined Dallas Street International Church. They helped her and soon she started working with them.

I was so proud of Emma. I actually agreed to come in to Dallas for free and do an event for the homeless people at the Dallas Street Church. That became a regular event for me.

Joe is one of the most creative artists I know and some of my marketing and promotional material you see in my social media are done by him. He's back in Dallas and we are still good friends.

I saved a baby's life and now I help save more lives.

We lived in Garden Grove, in Orange County, CA from 1987 until 1994 in a rented house. It was a very small two-bedroom town-house with a small yard. We got perfectly good, *free* furniture that people left in their front yards. Is this a great country, or what?

A Muslim family moved next to us. The man had a long beard and his wife had the hijab. They didn't talk to us. I don't know why. We were their neighbors, but for some reason they kept to themselves.

One time, minutes after I came back from work, we heard a woman screaming. Then she came to our front door and knocked repeatedly. I opened the door. It was our next- door neighbor. I didn't recognize her at first. She wasn't wearing her hijab. She was screaming in Arabic: "My baby. My baby!"

My mother and I ran to her house. The baby was not breathing. I called 911 and followed the operator's instructions on how to do basic CPR and to keep the baby's mouth open. My mom kept rubbing the baby's hands. Minutes later, the Garden Grove Fire Department arrived along with the Paramedics and took the baby to the nearest hospital. The mom jumped in the ambulance with them and we followed. Minutes later, the father arrived. I told him, in his language, that his baby was OK. After talking with the doctors and his wife, he came back out to the waiting room and thanked us for saving his son's life.

I wish I could tell you that our relationship as neighbors improved and we started having small talks, but it didn't. He went back to his quiet, shy ways and ignored us as usual.

Unlike our Mormon neighbor, Julie, who was so sweet to my family. She would bring my parents cookies and pies and she would visit them. I loved that, since I was gone all day and almost all night performing.

Julie attempted to invite my parents to her church and to give them the book of Mormon, but with no avail. They didn't care what angel personally talked to Joseph Smith. My parents are Greek Orthodox and planned to die Greek Orthodox.

Many years later, I started helping Crisis Pregnancy Centers raise money to continue their operations. We found out that laughter opens pockets. The centers found out that if they have me do comedy at their Galas and transition smoothly and "do the ask", people would give a lot more money than when they have their Directors do it.

I still love to save babies. I don't care what religion they are.

My Early Career

As I became permanent in my Accounting job, I had more time at night to work out. I joined 24-Hour Fitness and started exercising on a regular basis. I used to lift weights when I lived in Kuwait and it was nice to get back to that. I started running regularly. At the beginning, I could only run two miles since I had to stop and smoke a cigarette.

That's how I measured how far I ran; it was a personal achievement when I actually ran two whole cigarettes! Eventually I had to stop running. It was killing me!

One day, I had a crazy idea of running a marathon. It was crazy because the most I could run was one to two cigarettes, and to finish a marathon you need to run at least half a pack!

I signed up for the Los Angeles Marathon. I had no plans of finishing. I figured I'd run two miles that year, then build up to four the next year and so on.

The night before the Marathon, I was invited to a carb-loaded dinner offered by the City of Los Angeles. Mohammad Ali the boxer was there. I had the chance to meet him and shake his hand. He looked at me and softly said:

"You will finish this race, won't you?"

I lied and said timidly, "Yes sir, I will."

I went home that night and the next day, real early in the morning, I drove from Garden Grove to Los Angeles. There were thousands of people getting ready. I had to put a number on the front of my sleeveless white shirt. I felt like a prison inmate. I started looking at how some runners stretched before the race and copied them. I then went back to my car, smoked a cigarette and then joined the runners to start the race.

I heard the gun go off and started running. It was fun to run with thousands of people. Before I knew it, I was at the 3-mile mark. It was easier to run with other people. I made it to the 5-mile mark and my sides were hurting. I was at least two cigarettes behind.

I started slowing down and was ready to quit but other runners encouraged me to continue. I did. I kept running until the 10-mile mark. At that point, I was breathing like a woman giving birth. A few of the runners passing me said, "Keep running, it's downhill from here. It will get easier." I found out that day, that runners lie!

I kept walking and running and people on the side of the road kept cheering me on and asking me to continue. Some handed me cold water, others, watermelon, or popsicles. I kept asking everyone for a cigarette, but nobody handed me one.

I ran and walked until I got the 20th mile mark. Then when I thought my spleen was coming out of my mouth, my legs filed for a divorce and decided to leave me. I said that's enough. I'm done. Then an old homeless lady with raggedy clothes and a beautiful face looked at me and said: "Oh, No honey. You are almost there. You can't quit now."

I wasn't about to disappoint that homeless lady. I kept walking and running until I started seeing the finish line. I got my second wind, gave it my all, and passed the finish line!

I found a place on the ground and sat there with my lungs acting like an accordion. I was high on endorphins. I felt great. I had no one around to celebrate with. I just sat there, embarrassed to look at my feet. I didn't want to see what happened to them. I took my shoes off, and my toes immediately looked the other way. They were mad at me. They looked at me as if we were in a fight, and I left them and ran away, and they got beaten and bruised. I was in so much pain, I couldn't feel anything.

Despite my body's rebellion, I was so proud of myself. I didn't think I could push myself that far. I thought to myself. If I can do this, I can do *anything*.

I asked myself the following question: "What is it that I want to do in life, that if I never get paid for it, I'd still do it to the best of my ability?"

Making people laugh was my only response. I love to see people laugh.

I attempted to stand but my feet said, "No." I waited 15 more minutes then got up, walked to my car and drove home. My mom filled a big tub with warm salt water and I stuck my feet in and sat there for few hours.

I finished the twenty-six-point-two miles in 5:01:23 and my overall place was: 10,383. When the results were tallied, I believe the only person I beat was the old homeless lady.

The next day, I drove to the La Cabaret Comedy Club in Encino, CA. Encino is a neighborhood in the San Fernando Valley region of Los Angeles, California.

The club had an open-mic night. I signed up and waited. It was 7 PM and all the 300 seats of the comedy club were full. I waited and waited, with tens of other "up-and- coming" Comedians waiting their turn. By midnight they called me to the stage.

Compared to what it was earlier, now there were just 9 drunks left in the club. I was told I had 3 minutes, and when I saw the light in the back of the room, it was time for me to go to the stage.

Three minutes sounded like eternity for my first time on stage. I didn't have any jokes. I thought of all the little comments I made to people in the past that made them laugh.

Like when people asked me if I lived in a tent, when I lived in the Middle East, I would say: "Oh we lived in a two-story tent with a two-camel garage." I would add: "My brother used to go to my little sister's tent and steal her Ken and Barbie. I would then send G.I. Joe to get them back."

Also when asked about earthquakes in California, I would respond with: "The last one was so bad, I was at work, and the Slurpee machine fell and hit me on the head. I'm glad I had my turban on! Thank God, Larry H. Parker got me 2.1 million dollars!"

The drunk people loved my act. Two of them fell off their chairs laughing. I knew right there and then that I could do this. I was sure I had what it took to be a good Comedian.

The next day, I stood in line at the Laugh Factory on Sunset owned by an Iranian-Jew named Jamie Masada. Jamie was very kind to the comedians. I signed up but was not chosen to perform. They put up the old homeless lady instead. She was milking her Marathon win.

The next day I signed up at the famous Comedy Store on Sunset Blvd. in Hollywood, owned by Mitzi Shore — Pauly Shore's mother. That is the club that helped the careers of many comedians like Robin Williams, David Letterman, and Jim Carry. For the next few months club-hopping continued every single night.

I did hundreds and hundreds of open mic nights at coffee houses and restaurants. That's where Musicians and Artists come to play a song or two or do poetry to an audience comprised of other Musicians and Artists that want them to get off the stage, so they can perform. Occasionally there would be "qualified audience members" who were there to be entertained.

I remember at times that the venue would have two or three people in the audience and almost all of them were performers. Other times, there were two or three "qualified audience members", but they left following the performance of the Musician that came right before me. I used to sit in the back of the room and beg quietly: "Please don't go . . . I'm funny. I will make you laugh if you only stay." But they always ended up leaving before my three-minutes of comedy.

Many of the Comedians that were there left and never went on stage. Their excuse: "There was no real audience in the room. What's the use of performing to other Entertainers who are not listening?"

I did and performed at every opportunity and kept my ego in check, since I knew I had to perform to get better. And when I did get my opportunity to do the open mic nights at the real Comedy Clubs, I was ready with funny material.

Perseverance works. I had three jobs at the time and one of them was full time. I worked 7 days a week to make a living and still made time to do one or two open mic nights each night. I guess doing that Marathon inspired me in more ways than one.

At one time, I couldn't get a spot at the Comedy Store, so I stood in front of the line of people waiting to enter the Main Room of the Comedy Store and did a show for them. Yes, right there on the street!

Two security guards picked me up off the ground. Fortunately, they did it politely since they were laughing too, and the audience was enjoying my show.

I then drove to a Denny's restaurant with a fellow Comedian named Mark Scott, and I stood on one of tables and started doing my act. People weren't laughing in the beginning but eventually it happened. The whole restaurant became quiet and listened and laughed. The Manager came to me but waited for me to finish my act. He asked me to get down. I did. I thanked him for the great audience and left.

I can number many Comedians that started with me in these "Hell Gigs" as we called them. There were several who didn't feel the need to perform, and all of them are still in their day jobs wishing they could do comedy full time.

God Bless America. Perseverance works, and when you want something bad enough and you're willing to work hard for it, most likely *you can achieve it.*

I would come home from the comedy clubs around 1 AM or sometimes 2 AM, then fall directly into bed. The alarm would wake me up at 6 AM, I'd get ready, and drive to my daytime Accounting job in Irvine.

Once I got off at 5 PM, I would drive home, have dinner with my mom and dad, take a 20-minute nap, then drive to Los Angeles, Hollywood, Santa Monica, Pasadena or wherever there were slots available for me to perform. On Saturday mornings, I worked for my uncle's Subway sandwich shop and on Sunday I worked for the Baby Furniture store.

Believe me, it was all worth it. My career picked up so fast. After just a few months of performing at The Improv in Santa Monica, Mark Lonow, co-owner of the legendary Improvisation Comedy Club believed in me and asked me to become one of the new faces at the Improv. One of the few others that were chosen at the time was Sherry Shepherd (she was, until recently, one of the co-hosts at The View on TV).

That gave me a boost in my ego. I started working more clubs and did my first out-of- town gig; it was a new Comedy Club down-town Phoenix, Arizona. I was also featured at a Comedy Club in Palm Springs, CA that was owned by a lady named Phyllis. She used to work for Mitzi Shore, owner of the Comedy Store.

I remember one time I was performing at the Belly Room at the famous Comedy Store, a small 50-seater room, built on top of the Comedy Store. There were several Comedians in the room, one of whom happened to be Chris Rock. He was wearing a white suit. There were 5 guys sitting in the back and laughing so hard at my jokes. Once I got off the stage they all got up and walked up to me. It looked like one of them was a Celebrity and the rest were his Body Guards. He introduced himself as Bobby

Brown (he was married to the late singer Whitney Houston). He looked at me and said: "You're the funniest Comedian I've heard."

I started doing spots at the Iggy Comedy Store off Pico and the 10 freeway in Los Angeles and at the Pasadena Ice House.

That's when I was approached by Chuck Harris; my manager from Visual Arts Entertainment whom I mentioned earlier in this book.

Chuck once booked me at a club in North County San Diego where they were shooting a TV show for a new Comedy channel that was being launched by HBO. It was called Comedy Central. The segment that they shot of me was part of Stand-Up and *Short Attention Span Theater.*

The highest prestige I had was when I performed several times at the Melrose Improv Comedy Club. I remember one time I was so excited because I was given a spot at a great time at the club. That night, Adam Sandler showed up. I didn't know who he was but there were some Industry people that wanted to see him, so my spot was cancelled. I was bummed.

One of my favorite clubs to perform at was the Laugh Stop in Claremont, CA. Adam was the manager and he liked me. He gave me great spots. At one time, I became the opening act for a Hypnotist. I would get 15 minutes every Tuesday.

At that club, they did the Laugh Stop Comedy Competition. It was an annual Competition. One year I won the entire Competition. If my memory serves me, Kevin James from the Kings of Queens and Mall Cop, was one of the Contestants. I saw him again at a club right across the street from The Comedy and Magic Club in Hermosa Beach. Kevin was serious about his career. I really loved that. Some Comedians did comedy just to be noticed or seen by Industry people. They didn't care much about their act. Kevin James did, Andrew Dice Clay did. While other comics were drinking and using, some of us Comedians were busy working on our acts.

Another time, Virgin Airlines was getting introduced to the United States and they did a Comedy Competition with the finals at the Improv Comedy Club in Irvine, CA. Five Comedians made it to the finals. The judges were Alan Thick, Weird Al Yankovic and one other judge (Sorry, I don't remember his name). The prize was: You get to perform on the plane on Virgin Airline flights!

I didn't care about the prize. I wanted to win. At the end of the competition, they picked three of the five to perform on the Virgin Airlines flights. I was one of the winners out of a thousand Comedians. I immediately went home and started practicing demonstrating how to buckle a seat belt.

A week later, Saddam Hussein invaded Kuwait and they called the program off. I still have the apology letter from them saved somewhere. For some reason they didn't want a Middle Easterner to stand on the plane and tell jokes. Times haven't changed that much since.

One time, I was hired to open for Mr. B.B. King on New Year's Eve in Los Angeles. The concert hall was sold-out. People wanted to see Mr. B.B. King. When I was introduced, nobody was paying attention to me. But somehow, I wanted to prove myself. I started speaking louder, moving more on stage and got few people to listen. Once they listened, the laughter became contagious, and the rest of the crowd started listening and laughing. I finished with long applause from the audience.

During Intermission, I asked one of Mr. B.B. King's four Managers if I could say hello to Mr. King. A Manager jumped in and said, that Mr. B.B. King wanted to see me. I was then escorted to his green-room. He stood up when he saw me and told me that I was very funny and that he listened to some of my jokes. I was very impressed. I asked if I could take a picture with him. He said, "Wait, let me get Lucille (his guitar) in the picture!"

In my career, I've met many Celebrities, Mr. B.B. King was one of the kindest and humblest I ever had the pleasure to meet.

Speaking of demanding attention, many years later, I was booked to speak at a Coffee Association Banquet at the Ritz Carlton in Laguna Niguel, CA. I wasn't given many details about the gig. I thought it was only a small Association Banquet. I should've considered the fact that it was at the Ritz Carlton in Laguna Niguel.

When I arrived, I learned that anybody who was somebody in the coffee business was there. VP's of Starbucks, Coca Cola, and the CEO of Coffee Bean and Leaf. Also, Coffee Bean Farm owners from all over the world. With 300 people in attendance, you could smell money and coffee in that room.

I was introduced by the Master of Ceremonies and no one paid attention. They kept talking and talking. I didn't want to go for another 30 minutes of struggle on stage, so I resorted to "Jungle Mentality". If you attack the Leader, the Pride will respect you. I knew it was a huge risk, but I wasn't about to let 300 millionaires ruin my show.

I proceeded to ask one of the audience members that was listening: "Who is the wealthiest man here? Who has the most influence?" He pointed to a Brazilian Farms owner at a table in the center of the banquet hall. I asked for his name and that audience member gave it to me.

I then called his name out. The whole room stopped. I said, "Hello Sir, how are you?"

He looked up and said, "Hello".

I then asked him: "Are you an illegal immigrant?"

He laughed hard and said, "No. I live in Brazil."

I then said, "So you grow coffee beans?"

He said: "Yes."

I said, "Why, is that because you don't know how to play soccer?"

He laughed hard and that was it. The room was mine for the rest of the show. I picked on the Coca Cola CEO and everyone in the room was afraid to talk, so I didn't pick on them.

It worked. I then shared with the Starbucks VP that I was a big fan of Starbucks and that I LOVED Starbucks. I told him that I bought Starbucks coffee every day.

Following the show, everyone came and shook my hand. Including the Brazilian farmer and his entourage.

The VP of Starbucks came shook my hand and thanked me for being a loyal customer. And he then left!

"What? No gift certificates? No free coffee for life? What's going on?" I said to myself. "I gave his company the biggest advertisement."

Seconds later, the CEO of The Keurig Company, which was unheard of back then, introduced himself and asked for my address.

A few weeks later, Fedex dropped a huge box in front of my house. It had the first Keurig machine and 500 K-Cups along with a tray and other things.

Guess what I started drinking from that point on?

I actually convinced many of my friends to buy their coffee machine and started buying them myself and giving them as Home Warming gifts to friends and family.

I share all this not to brag, but to let you know that my potential was there and with dedication and practice, things looked very promising.

This picture, with my mom, was taken 23 years ago in Malibu right before my show at the Whisky a Go-Go, the world-famous Rock & Roll club in Hollywood. The Doors, Janis Joplin, and Led Zeppelin have performed there to name a few.

Why would they let a Comedian perform there? Because I persisted and kept asking. I wanted a place to perform on the Sunset Strip, when some of the Comedy Clubs didn't have room for an up and coming Comedian.

This picture reminds me of persistence. When you persist, doors open. I lost my hair and my waist since, but I still have my mom, my sense of humor, and my persistence.

Persist. Don't give up. It will pay off.

I learned that from running the Marathon. I wasn't aware of my potential. I wasn't aware that I could go further than I thought I could; expect more of myself than usual; and push myself regardless of how I feel.

It not only works with sports or running Marathons, but it works with life itself. With your career, your goals, your relationships.

In your career: You might think you are only smart enough and capable enough of getting to a Supervisory level, but you can, if you push yourself, become a Manager or a VP or even a CEO. Why not? You have the potential.

In your marriage, you can, with God's help, continue to draw closer to your spouse than you thought possible. You do have the potential to become a great husband or a great wife.

As a Comedian, I knew I had the potential. It was just a matter of pushing myself to accomplish my goal. Yes, I suffered from a lack of sleep, missed opportunities to hang out with friends and movies that I didn't have the time to go see since I was busy working on my craft, but I don't regret any of that. I was willing to sacrifice everything to accomplish my goal. I'm glad I did.

I'm always amazed how God can use our past experiences and the trials we go through to bless other people. As an example, I never thought that my experience with Captain the drug dealer, at Joe's party, would give me experience to deal with inmates at prisons, homeless people at shelters, and addicts. But God surprised me. If you give Him the opportunity, He'll surprise you as well.

Get ready to be encouraged...

CHAPTER 4

RESCUED FROM MY OWN DREAM

The First Hope in 24 Hours

When I think about and remember how
There was no way out and You rescued me
There's no reason why
You loved me then and You love me now
Least, no reason I can see

You had always been my closest friend
Even though I'd never defended that
I was so far away
As far as ever I could stray
But You were there to bring me back

Thank You Jesus
For the grace that You have given us
We could never repay
But from my heart I'd like to say That I thank You

THANK YOU JESUS LYRICS—TERRY CLARK

I was once performing at the Ice House Comedy Club in Pasadena, CA. I finished my show, ordered a drink and was watching a Japanese Comedian doing his act. He was funny. He was also clean. Didn't cuss, didn't throw the "F" bomb. After he got off the stage, I commended him and offered him a drink. He said he didn't drink.

We talked for a while. His name is YAMO—short for Yamawaki. At that time, I didn't know that this person would become one of my best friends. After a short conversation, He asked me if I'm a Christian. I said: "Yes. Of course. I'm from the Holy Land. We gave the world Jesus. We gave you all major religions."

When you think about it, the Middle East gave America religion, oil, convenience (711 stores and gas stations). Lately we gave America Home Land Security.

I can't think of any other people who gave more. What have the French given America? The Statue of Liberty! What have the Italians given America? The Mafia and Pizza.

What have the Chinese given America? Walmart. I'm exaggerating here of course. It is just a joke.

I wore a cross. All my life. I wore it in Kuwait. Some Muslim kids were not thrilled by it. But I didn't care. Christianity was my identity. That was the first thing you try to figure out in the Middle East when you meet a person for the first time. You hope you can find out without asking.

When a Middle Easterner meets another Middle Easterner, there are ways for him or her to find out if that person is a Christian or a Muslim. First from the name. If your name is Mohamed, Ahmed, or Ishmael you are a Muslim. If your name is George, Elias or Gabi, you are a Christian. But there are names like Emad, Abdullah or Samir; you can't tell. Some Christians deliberately give their kids names that you cannot tell if they are Christians. Especially in persecuted areas of the Middle East.

If you can't find someone's faith from their name, you could tell from their last name, their dad's name, or the words they use when they talk.

Christianity was a culture for me. It was a label. We didn't go to church. There was a Greek-Orthodox church in Kuwait, but my parents never forced us to go. My parents were not religious. Once a year, the priest would come to our apartment and he would be wearing a black robe with a black head cover and had a long black beard. When he walked into the house, my dad would bow and kiss his hand. My mom would do the same. That was difficult for her to do. Submission was not in her DNA. Then my dad would call us boys, and we had to kiss the priest's hand and the cross he carried. That act affected me. Till this day, every time I watch the Duck Dynasty show or meet a person with a long beard, I cross my heart and say, "Forgive me Father. I have sinned."

The priest would them walk into every room in our apartment, holding a wet plant in his hand and would chant and splash the walls with water. It was supposed to keep the evil spirits out of the home. Dad would then hand the priest money and he went home.

Mom complained about the stains on the walls. As for me, I'd rather have stained walls than demons in my room.

I once received a package in the mail that had the Bible book of John in it. It was sent from somewhere in America. I don't remember all the details, but I recall it had a Bible study and questions. Every time I filled it out and sent it back, they would send me another book. I did that for a while then stopped. All they ever sent me were books of the Bible. I kept hoping for something like "Cat in The Hat."

My point in all this is that, while I was surrounded by Christianity, it never really sunk in. I was, at best, a "cultural Christian". While it defined me, other than our occasional wet walls, it didn't affect my life one way or the other.

Something interesting that I could've never figured out, is that I never called God's name in vain. Even in my darkest days, I've never called God's name in vain. I never cursed using God's name. Many people around me did, but I never did.

Well, Yamo was persistent and asked me to go to church with him. That Sunday, I had the day off and went to his church. It was the Southern Baptist Church of La Habra, CA.

When we arrived, I went inside with him. The church had nothing on the walls. Just a cross and pews. I told Yamo that they need to hire a gay Catholic Interior Designer to add some pizzazz to the church. He tried to explain that the church is not a building, but the people are the church.

There was no incense, no icons, and no oil—just people singing from a hymn book. Later, the Pastor, Dr. Randy Stoval, a stocky muscular man in his 30s, wearing a brown suit came up and started teaching. He was talking about tithing. I didn't understand what he was talking about. Yamo looked at me and while sinking in his seat, said: "I brought you to the wrong service." I said: "No, I'm OK I like him. I like his authority." He said: "Don't worry. It's his last week. He is moving to a different church."

When we left that day, I didn't feel anything spiritual. But almost without my knowing, a seed had been planted.

I went to my day job at the Restaurant Enterprise the next day. The company owned over 2000 restaurants, and my department oversaw the Payroll Taxes for them. I finished my Accounting studies while I was in California and took the Certified Payroll Professional exam. My job was critical. If we forgot to pay the government on time, my company would have to pay huge penalties. I did a good job. I was "Employee of the month" several times. I liked the people that worked in the Tax Department with me and we partied every weekend. Another Japanese temp once took an hour to share Jesus with me. I brushed him off.

A few other people from my company were trying to share Jesus with me. I don't know why. I was a nice guy. I'm a Christian. I went to a Scientology meeting by myself one time, in Orange County. They wanted me to take a cleansing sauna and attend more classes. That was the end of it for me with Scientology. They were pressuring me to take their personality test. I know I have a personality. Why should I fill out a form to prove it to them?

I attended a mid-week service with Yamo at Calvary Chapel Pacific Hills. Pastor Rick was very funny. He could pass for a Comedian. I felt like God was after me. One time I was at an Alpha Beta grocery store in Garden Grove where I lived at the time. The cashier looked at me and said, "You need Jesus."

What was going on? I'll tell you what it was — God was after me! That Sunday, my friend Yamo was out of town. I decided to locate where Pastor Randy moved to and try to attend that church.

I found out that he was preaching at a church on Redhill in Tustin, CA. I went to the service there that Sunday morning. I wore a jacket this time and some slacks. I got to the church. I was a little late. The service just started. One old Deacon stopped me at the entrance of the Sanctuary and said, "Hey, can you tuck your long hair under the jacket? I had long hair back then. I miss it.

I said, "No. I will not." I'm still a Comedian and has the rebellious mentality. He said, "Then, can you sit in the back here with the Ushers." I replied, "Fine. I came here to see Dr. Randy."

Until that moment, I felt God was mad at me. I knew He

knew my sinful thoughts, my drug use, my drinking, and my past. Although, I didn't think about it, it burdened me subconsciously. It felt like a ton of bricks on my back. If you asked me what is the cross that I was wearing meant, I couldn't tell you.

I sat there next to the Ushers holding their tithing bags. The Tax Collectors. Just kidding.

I can't tell you what Dr. Randy was teaching on, but at the end of the service, He asked if anyone wanted to give his or her life to Christ. If anyone wanted to have their sins forgiven, to have their guilt taken away, that they should come forward to the alter. I ran forward crying. I was the only one. It was embarrassing now that I think about it, butI didn't care. That emptiness I felt all along was being filled as I started seeking God. I stood there and repeated a prayer with Dr. Randy. He then said, "Welcome to the Family of God." The congregation applauded.

Dr. Randy asked me if I wanted to get baptized. I said, "I'm pretty sure they did that when I was a baby, but why not." As I walked back to the back of the church, many strangers hugged and congratulated me. I didn't know any of them, but some of them became family to me. Some are still friends to this day. The old Deacon who wanted me to tuck my hair in my jacket, gave me a hug and congratulated me. He said, "Welcome brother. I like your hair."

What a difference a day makes. 24 little hours. That was the slogan of an old Men's Warehouse commercial, but it was so true for how I felt that day. I felt fulfilled. I felt like a burden was taken away from me. I somehow felt like I was on God's side now.

I went home that day and told my mom what happened. What a surprise; she frowned. She said: "We are Greek Orthodox. What is wrong with you? Why would you change your religion?"

We used to have a neighbor in Kuwait who was like you, Born Again."

That became my label by my family for a while. Why are you Born Again? Why did you leave the Greek Orthodox faith? I didn't leave anything. I wasn't on one team and moved to another. I left filth, emptiness, guilt and started seeking God.

For the next few years, I had to deal with this issue with some of my relatives. I became the guy involved in the Cult. The outsider. All of a sudden, they all became experts in the Bible that they never opened and started telling me how wrong I was. To their credit, many years later, I gained their respect and we agreed on more things than what we disagreed on.

In the Middle East, you can disagree with your family, get loud and scream at each other, but at the end of the day, you are family. It's OK to disagree.

Life changed for me in 24 hours. I had no desire to smoke, to drink, to go to a party. I loved everybody and all I wanted to do is read the Bible. Seven days a week. I went to church 5 times that week. I was hungry for God.

And then I made the CALL . . . .

It was on Monday that I called my manager Chuck Harris. He thought it was just a typical call to talk about my career or to inquire about a gig he booked me at, but he noticed my voice was different.

I said, "Chuck. I know you believe in me and you helped me, but I think I'm quitting."

"Quitting what?" He replied.

"Quitting comedy!" I said

"What?" He answered shockingly.

"Yes. I want to quit comedy!" I firmly answered.

"Why?" he asked.

"You might not understand Chuck, as a Jewish person, but I'm a Christian now," I said.

"You were always a Christian, Nazareth!" Chuck answered with a confused tone.

"Yes, but I'm a *real* Christian now and I can't honor God by doing comedy." I explained.

He said, "Look at Brad Stine (his other client). He's a Christian and he still does clubs."

I persisted and said, "Yes, I really want to quit comedy."

"But what about the sitcom and the shows?" Chuck replied with a frustrated tone.

"I will finish up the dates I have and then quit." I assured him.

"Are you sure you are not going with any other management?" he suspiciously asked.

"No, I'm not. I'm quitting." I replied firmly.

There were few "F" words and other curses that were said to me in between but after Chuck hung up on me, I knew I did the right thing.

Everything I dreamt about was before me. But I knew I had to focus on what God wanted from me.

I had one show left at the Improv in Irvine (Back then it was near University of California, Irvine Campus). My Pastor at the time, Randy Stoval, wanted to bring a group from the church and come see me perform. I refused and told him that although I cleaned up my act, there are other comics that night that would not hold to that standard.

Pastor Randy suggested doing a Comedy Night at the church. Remember, this was 1992. I agreed and started preparing the Fellowship Hall to turn it into a Comedy Club. My friend Yamo helped me and, the night of the show, I invited my friend Brad Stine to perform as well. That night almost 400 people showed up uninvited. I had one of the best performances of my career.

Right before the show, Pastor Randy and few Deacons prayed for me. One old Deacon prayed the following: "God, use Nazareth's comedy for your Glory!"

I will never forget that prayer. It has been engraved in my brain ever since.

That night of comedy turned into the Christian Comedy Club at Red Hill Church. The first Christian Comedy Club in the Country at the time. We had t-shirts made, we had people serving food and drinks (Christian drinks, that is). It lasted for two years but it was ahead of its time.

Many years later, I started another Comedy Club called the Comedy Place at Sunrise in Rialto, CA. That one had waiters and waitresses and a cover charge. We did well for two years before we finally closed it down.

God was so quick to let me know what He wanted from me. I'm so glad it included Comedy. While I've had several other jobs in my life, when I do comedy, I feel as if I'm doing the thing I do best. I love comedy. I love performing, but I was willing to give it up for God.

I'm so glad he didn't ask me to give it up. I was willing to sacrifice the one thing that meant the most to me but, thank God, He had other plans. Otherwise I'd still be delivering baby furniture on Sundays!

CHAPTER 5
DAD WANTED ME TO GO!

I didn't know much about anemia. It claimed my father's life. In the last year of his life, we didn't know what was wrong with him. He felt very tired, was pale and had no appetite. After months of tests and going to one doctor after the other, one doctor finally discovered his problem.

He said: "Your dad needs some blood."

"What do you mean?" I asked. This doctor was calling my dad a vampire.

He advised me to take my dad to the hospital and there, have the medical staff give him two bags of blood. He said: "He'll be fine."

My father had dentures and he was ready for new ones. They cost around 2000 dollars. The thought of getting him the dentures from the Halloween shop became appealing.

They only cost $2, and he could get blood for free. But I'd have to drive him around at night.

But seriously, we went to Hoag Hospital in Newport Beach, and they gave him two bags of blood. After they finished the blood transfusion, my father felt lively again. From out of the jaws of death, he was back to normal.

What a miracle. My father was well again, his cheeks were rosy, he was feeling great and eating everything my mother told him not to.

Few weeks later, my dad started to feel tired and pale again. Oh no. "Dad, are you leaking?" I thought to myself, "What's going on?"

We went back to the doctor and he said that we need to take him back to the hospital and do the blood transfusions again. He also informed me that we needed to do so on a regular basis.

So, it became a routine for me and Dad: I take him to the hospital; we pull up to the super-unleaded pump, (well, it's like an IV tube) and I wait for him to finish. It was a nice time to spend with dad. To just sit and talk. I always asked him if he needed a car wash with his fill up.

As strange as it may seem, this became a fun thing to do for me and dad. I even asked the doctor if they could install a blood gauge on my dad's forehead, so I could tell when he was on empty. After all, I didn't want to see my dad stranded in the middle of the road.

What I was not aware of is that you cannot do blood transfusions forever. The human body can only take so many. After a few times, the body will start rejecting it. I was shocked when the doctor told me the bad news.

"What do you mean doctor?" I asked.

"What I mean is your dad will have to survive on the blood he has until his organs stop."

"You mean die?" I gasped.

"Yes. There is not much we can do, sir," was the doctor's reply.

I pleaded with the doctor to give him one more blood transfusion, at my consent, and I'd take all responsibility. That meant two more weeks to spend with Dad. I had a hard time getting it through my head; baring a miracle, my father's life was going end, and soon!

Two weeks later we were back in the hospital. This time he had to stay. There was nothing else we could do but wait for his blood to run short and his organs to start stopping one after the other.

After a few days, they moved him to a different hospital in Costa Mesa, California called College Hospital. The plan was to comfort him the last week of his life.

That was when I prayed my dad out of this life. I asked Christ to take him before his organs shut down.

The night dad died, I was with him in the hospital. His breathing was not doing good. His blood pressure was very low. My dad was not awake. He was on morphine. I looked at him and said: "Dad, I have a show to do tonight. I'm going to leave you for two hours.

There are people waiting for me there. I will be back. Please don't die till I get back."

I drove to the show with tears in my eyes. I wanted to be with my dad when he transitioned from this life to meet the Lord. I know my dad accepted Christ in the last eight months we spent together going back and forth to and from Hoag hospital.

It was easy to show dad that we are saved not by our good works but by faith in what Jesus did for us on the Cross. My dad was in a hospital bed. He couldn't do much good work. He didn't have any money to give to the poor, he couldn't do any good works that could save him. He knew the fragility of man! I shared the Hope of Jesus with Him.

We talked about Eternal life and what the Bible says in the famous verse: John 3:16 "For God so loved the World that He gave His only son, that who so ever believes in Him should not be eternally dead but have ever lasting life."

My dad knew I meant what I said. Even after his years of my family mocking my faith, my dad knew that I was a Christian. It was pretty obvious. He saw my old life. He knew how immoral I was.

I'm ashamed to admit it now, but one time when he lived with me in Ohio, I took him to a strip club. He didn't want to go, but I insisted. I ordered him a bottle of whiskey and paid the dancer to dance on our table. While the dancer was performing for my dad, I picked up a little tube where I kept my cocaine. I made few lines right on the table where the stripper was dancing, rolled a dollar bill and snorted it right in front of the entire bar. My friend Lee, and the rest of the entourage started looking around nervously and called me crazy. Dad was very uncomfortable, but he never said "no" tome.

Another time, while working at the fish house that I started, I challenged one of my workers to a drinking contest. I wanted to see who could drink a case of beer the fastest! Not just a single beer. Oh, no, I had to bet on an entire case! That's just my personality; go big or go home.

What we did was, take a knife, cut a hole on the bottom of the can, then put it to your mouth and open the can. Beer shot directly into your stomach. In hindsight, I can honestly say, I don't recommend this.

My memory's a little fuzzy, but I think I won. Frankly, I don't remember anything after the 10th can. My mom told me that dad picked me up while I laid flat on the lawn in front of the store, took me to the house and laid me on the bed.

My parents knew that when I asked Christ into my life, it was a radical change. No one could question the authenticity of my faith. They saw the results.

As I arrived at the show, the Promoter was happy to see me. He was trying some of his jokes on me. People think that Comedians are always in a good mood. That for some reason we're always ready to tell jokes on demand.

The truth is most Comedians I know, are serious people. Dramatic people. We spend our days observing people and observing life. We are not always funny and ready to make people laugh. We call those Comedians who can do that "Clowns".

I went into the green room, that's the room entertainers wait in until show time. Most of the time, it is behind the stage. Back in the day, the Comedy Store on Sunset Blvd. in Hollywood, CA had a room that Comedians waited in to go on stage. It had green walls, but I'm sure Wikipedia has a different explanation of why they call it the Green Room.

I sat there, going over my jokes. I didn't want to try anything new. I just wanted to finish my obligation and rush back to the hospital.

I was introduced, I went on stage, and for the next hour I was crying inside. I was thinking of all the good times I had with my dad, as few as they were.

My dad worked hard. He wasn't home much. Every Friday, which at the time, was the only day off in Kuwait, dad worked. He would take me to work with him. While he was in the office finishing paperwork, I found things to keep me busy and entertained. Dad never played ball with me. He never played video games with me. He was busy working.

Dad had American and British friends at the Embassies in Kuwait that were able to get him some Johnny Walker whiskey. He liked whiskey. He also smoked Rothman's English cigarettes. Four packs a day to be exact. As a youngster, I used to walk to the store next to our apartment and buy him cigarettes. There were no laws in Kuwait in the 70's that prevented children from buying cigarettes.

I remember times, when mom and dad were out, I would pour a glass of whiskey for myself and smoke a cigarette or two. I was 13 when I started smoking. I didn't have to worry. Cigarettes were everywhere around the house. Especially at Christmas and Easter. It was the custom that the neighbors visit you on your holidays. The Muslim neighbors would visit us during Christmas and Easter and we would visit them during their Adha and Fitr Eids. When they'd visit, we'd offer them Turkish Coffee, some holiday cookies and . . . cigarettes.

Mom would send me to the store, a day before each holiday, and I would buy 10 different brands of cigarettes. I could choose the brands. So, at an early age I experimented with many different cigarettes. My favorite was Marlboro reds. I never owned a horse, I didn't know what a cowboy looked like, but Marlboro tasted the best for me.

People connected based on the brand of cigarettes they smoked. If you went to a job interview and the interviewer smoked the same brand you did, chances are you'd get the job. It was like a club. The Marlboro club, the Kent Club, and the Dunhill club, etc. Funny, they didn't have Camel cigarettes in Kuwait!

Since dad smoked at home, it was not a big deal to hide the smell. To be honest, everybody smoked indoors back then. Our home had a constant cloud of smoke hanging close to the ceiling. Occasionally, a shepherd with his goats and sheep would pass by on our street and his goats smoked. Yes, I'm serious. In the middle of the city, shepherds still passed through with their flock.

I was never resentful of my dad for not spending time with me. He was providing for the family. There were no Psychologists at the time telling him to spend more time with his wife and kids. We turned out to be normal. Well, my two older brothers did. They are married with kids and Engineering Degrees and running a normal life. I guess that makes me the black sheep.

Back to my show. While I was on stage, I'd occasionally look at the audience and they'd be laughing and applauding. It was surreal. I had to keep reminding myself to smile.

Once I finished my last joke, I thanked the audience, grabbed the check and ran out of the club and back to College Hospital in Costa Mesa, CA where my dad was fighting for his life.

Now, performing while my dad was so near death may seem callous to you, but I always honor my commitments and this booking was no different. I can't cancel an engagement just because I don't "feel" funny. Being a Comedian is my job and I take it seriously.

Regardless, I came close to backing out of this one. Had my gig been out of town, I really don't know what I would have done.

I arrived at the hospital and ran into the room. The machines were still on. The beeping sounded so sweet. I remember times when I spent hours in the hospital room with him, listening to the beeping sound. The minute it changed, I would jump up and call the nurse.

I looked down at the frail body lying in the bed. My father was still unconscious. I thanked him for waiting for me. I prayed to God to take him right then, before the other organs stopped. The night shift Doctor, a short balding man with glasses, wearing a white coat over his shirt and tie, came to my dad's room and assured me that dad would not die anytime soon.

I went home. We only lived about 10 minutes away. When I got home, mom asked me how dad was doing. I told her what the Doctor told me.

That night I couldn't sleep. I went to my room and just stared at my computer. A few minutes later, I got a call. It was from the Doctor. He said, "I'm sorry. Your dad's heart stopped few minutes ago. He went in his sleep under the influence of morphine with no pain."

I said, "Amen. Thank you, Lord, for answering my prayers."

He said, "What?" I said, "Never mind, thank you for calling me Doctor, I will be there in few minutes."

I told mom and didn't have time to see her reaction. Mom was a tough woman. She didn't cry easily. I got to the hospital. My dad was lying there in the bed, with a peaceful look on his face. No machines, no wires, no pain. Death can take pain away. Death can take suffering away, but it can't take memories away. It can't take away the love you have for that loved one.

I sat on the chair looking at him. I opened my Bible and started reading verses where God gives us hope in the afterlife. I had a peace that I couldn't explain. It was just like the Bible says—it passed my understanding. Even though I prayed for God to end my father's suffering, I couldn't understand why I wasn't sad.

I was happy that God had answered my prayer. I kept reading the Bible while I waited for the funeral home to send someone to pick up my dad's body.

While I was waiting there in the room reading the Bible, dad's arm moved! Then his body moved!

A bad word came out of my mouth suddenly. I thought, "Oh, no. My dad is still alive. Oh no. Dad rose from the dead! Really Lord? You would do that for me? You would raise my dad from the dead!"

I ran down the hall, called the nurse. I said, "Come, quick! My dad is still alive. He just moved!" She came running, looked at him and said. "Oh, I'm sorry. I forgot to turn the mattress off. We have mattresses that moves every few minutes so that the patient doesn't get bed sores." She said, "Your dad is still dead!"

Oh, how I wished he would've stayed alive and healthy to see me become successful. To meet my wife and see my kids. To play with my kids. Dad loved children. He would squeeze their cheeks all the time. But God wanted him more than we did. I'm thankful that I could spend the last few years of his life with him. Especially the last eight months sitting beside his bed talking about his life.

One day, while at that hospital, my dad told me about his life when he lived in Gaza, Palestine. He was born in 1929. He never finished High School. He had a fight with one of his teachers; called him a bad word then left school. His dad was a Gold Merchant.

He bought and sold gold. He told me that some of these merchants would go to Egypt, buy gold coins, swallow them and then drive across the border into Gaza. They'd make it through customs without paying the tariff and then, use your imagination here, retrieve the gold coins, boil them in water and sell them. If the merchant forgot what he was carrying and flushed the toilet before he retrieved the coins, he'd literally flush his profits down the drain! Oh, and as a word of caution; I'm not saying they still practice this, but when buying gold in the Middle East, don't ever bite down on a coin!

Eventually my dad learned how to be a Jeweler. So, he didn't have to swallow any precious metals, he took the gold, melted it, and shaped it into rings, bracelets and necklaces. He was very good at what he did. As I said, he owned a Jewelry store in the Gaza strip.

Dad said to me that day: "Son, when I die, I want you to go to Gaza. There is a family home that we own. I want you to change my ownership of the home into your mother, your brother's and your name." I told him I would do that for him.

Dad's funeral was simple. All my cousins from Northern California and North Carolina, my aunt and cousins from San Diego, my aunts from Washington State, all came to the funeral. My dad was buried in Tustin, California. My brother, Ramzi from Kuwait also made it to the funeral.

We didn't want an open casket. I hated the fact that in this country, they put make-up on the deceased. I didn't want my last memory of my dad to be with him with lipstick and rosy cheeks. When I first learned that they put make-up on deceased people, I asked to be cremated when I die. "Take my ashes and sprinkle them over Home Depot or Dodgers Stadium. Not over a flower field."

Following the funeral and the prayer at the graveyard, everyone left the hall to go eat.

Boy, Americans sure love to eat. They'll take any excuse or

lame reason to eat out. Valentine's day is not about love; it's about going out and eating. Let me prove my point. Imagine you don't take your loved one out to dinner on Valentine's Day. It does not count. Something is wrong. How about not taking your Mom out to dinner on Mother's Day. Do you get the point? Americans make up holidays just to go out and eat.

Even the day you and I die, our family will go eat in memory of us. It's all about food.

After the family left to go eat, my friend Yamo and I stayed to watch the funeral home workers bury the casket. It was about noon. It was very hot outside. Sunny with no wind. Once the workers left, Yamo and I, bowed our heads and I prayed.

I asked God to give me a sign that my dad was in Heaven with Him. Suddenly, and for few seconds, the wind blew so hard and so peacefully, we almost fell on our backs. I know this sounds Pentecostal, but I do have a witness to this. Yamo is the one that keeps reminding me of that moment. I never again doubted that my dad is in Heaven.

I hope by reading this chapter, you'll know that God loves you, regardless of how bad you think you are or were. My life was changed in 24 hours.

Even if your earthly dad was too busy for you or not present in your life, you have a Heavenly Father who loves you and Has a plan for your life. His plan for me was much better than what Hollywood planned for me.

I surrendered my plans to God. The most important thing for me at that time was my career, my dream. I obediently surrendered all for Him.

But God had a different plan. You'll see what he had in mind in the next chapters.

CHAPTER 6:

I'M STARVING . . . .
LET'S DO IT!

The Second Hope in 24 Hours

I'll admit I wasn't the happiest traveler on that 18-hour KLM flight from Los Angeles Airport to Ben Gurion Airport in Israel. I really didn't want to go back to Israel at that time. I was building my career as a Comedian in the faith-based market and, to my mind, this was an irritating delay. As you'll soon see, our plans and God's plans don't always coincide.

The flight landed, and I trudged out of the plane, down the stairs and found my way to the shuttle bus that would take us to the terminal. Once I touched the ground, a plethora of emotions overtook me. This was my land. The Holy Land. I was born there but, strangely, I didn't feel as if I belonged. My home was

Newport Beach, CA. My identity was as an American. I know I wasn't born in the USA, but I was now officially true red, white, and blue!

I was taken aside by the Israeli customs and interrogated for one hour for the purpose of my coming to Gaza. You must admit it looked a little suspicious; I was a single man in his early 30's coming to visit Israel.

I started sharing with the Israeli soldier about the Lord Jesus. Since he was Jewish, it really sped up the process. The guy just wanted me out of his way as quickly as possible.

Once I came out into the arrivals area outside, I had no problem finding a taxi that was willing to take me to the Eritz checkpoint in Gaza. The best part of the ride was that this taxi driver didn't try to rip me off!

It was an hour drive in the desert from Ben Gurion Airport to Eritz checkpoint. It seemed longer because of the long flight.

I arrived at Eritz checkpoint around 9 AM. The taxi dropped me in front of the Eritz Gate. I took my luggage and walked into the checkpoint. I handed the Israeli soldier my American Passport. I was a proud American, but I looked Palestinian. I was very friendly with the soldier. I told him that I was from Southern California. He said, He studied in San Francisco, CA. We had small talk about the Dodgers and the Giants but the rest of the soldiers around him still gave me suspicious looks.

Jews:

You must understand my struggle. I grew up in Kuwait. We were taught to hate the Jews. Not just the Israelis but the Jews in general.

We learned it in school. We watched it on TV and it was communicated clearly to us.

Everything that went wrong with the Middle East was blamed on the Jews. If two Arabs fought, it was the Jew's fault. If we had bad weather, it was the Jew's fault for they controlled the weather. In Kuwait we drank Pepsi, because Coca Cola was not allowed to be imported to Kuwait, because it was dealing with Israel (Does that mean Pepsi didn't?)

We drove Chevys and Cadillacs, but not Fords. Ford dealt with Israel. The sad part was, we believed it. I never knew the impact of learning to hate anybody or any group will have on you.

As I came to this Country and started doing comedy. I was surrounded by Jews. Most club owners were Jews. Mitzi Shore, from the Comedy Store, Jewish. Bud Friedman, co-owner of the Improv Comedy Clubs . . . . Jewish. Jaimie Masada, owner of the Laugh Factory . . . . Iranian Jew.

Most of the comics I worked with were Jewish. They were the kindest people. Mark Lonow, the other owner of the Improv Comedy Clubs, who gave me my first break . . . . Jewish. My manager, Chuck Harris . . . . . . Jewish.

It wasn't until I gave my life to Christ and God changed my heart to love people that any hate that was left for the Jews was removed. I was filled with love, not just for the Jews, but for all people.

Many years later, I toured with a wonderful Rabbi named Bob Alper. A great man. A funny man. The name of the tour was One Arab, One Jew. Comedy for Peace.

We had so much fun during that tour. We laughed and laughed. We spoke at different Universities around the Country. We promoted peace.

That Is my prayer, that Palestinian and Israeli children can grow up together with love and peace and learn love instead of hate. Is that possible? I'm not sure. I leave it to the Prince of Peace to handle it!

I made it through the checkpoint and walked until I got to the Palestinian side. My cousin, Hatem, from Baltimore, was waiting there for me on the Palestinian side of the checkpoint.

Hatem

Growing up in Kuwait, we lived close to my cousin Hatem. He was two years older than me, but my brothers and I enjoyed hanging out with him. Hatem was a smart kid. I always looked up to him. His mom, Layla, was my dad's sister and that was the only home my mom allowed us to spend the night at occasionally. It was a big deal for us to spend the night outside the home. Mom was very protective and fearful, so we were not allowed to hang out with friends past 8 PM.

A few years later, Hatem and his family moved to Jordan and we lost touch until we met again many years later in San Francisco at a cousin's wedding. It felt like we were never separated. We caught up fast.

Hatem had one problem. He was an Atheist. But to his credit, he was one of the nicest, most honest, and moral person I knew. He was better than many Christian friends I knew. That was very confusing to me. When Hatem gave you his word, it was as good as gold. He helped so many people. He was also a very successful Engineer.

We spent many hours discussing faith issues. We always ended up agreeing not to agree. He knew I was praying for him. In 2011,

Hatem found out he had colon cancer. We visited him while he was going through chemo therapy. At that time, the arguments stopped and when he dropped me at the airport, it was the last time I saw him alive, he asked me to pray for him. I told him that I was.

A few months later, Hatem died at age 51. At his funeral, the mayor of Maryland, Martin O'Malley, showed up to the funeral. So many people that were impacted by Hatem's life were there.

When I looked at Hatem laying in the casket, I knew there was no Atheist lying there. He was touched by God.

Hatem left two boys, Zayd and Yousef. There were 14 and 13 at the time he died. I love these two boys. I continued to visit them to just be a father figure as needed. They regularly attended church and were involved with their local church.

Back to my story. Hatem arrived from Baltimore few days earlier preparing for his wedding. A year earlier, he had come to Gaza and had met a young girl named Nuha.

He asked her parents for her hand in marriage and they agreed. They started courting but they did most of it over the phone since he lived in Baltimore, Maryland.

Hatem was excited to show me his bride. He showed me pictures of her a few weeks earlier while I was visiting my aunt, his mom, in Baltimore.

His mom, Layla, was sad for the loss of my dad, her brother. When Hatem found out I was going down to Gaza, he asked if I would like to be the best man at his wedding. I gladly accepted. We spent hours talking about his fiancée, Nuha. He loved her and was excited for the wedding.

When Hatem saw me coming out of Eritz, we hugged like the long-lost friends we were, and he drove me directly to the house where my dad grew up. It was still owned by our family and most of my cousins had flown down to attend the wedding. The house was full of people. I saw cousins that I haven't seen for over 20 years. Hatem was in a rush to take me to meet Nuha.

A few months before my dad's death, he received a call from an old friend named, Yousef. Yousef was also dad's relative. They hadn't seen each other in over 30 years. They were best friends and close cousins. That phone call lasted for almost an hour. That month, Yousef died of a heart attack. My dad died few months later. My mom insisted that when I get to Gaza, I should go to Aya, his widow, and send our condolences.

It was on my list of things to do.

We got into the car and drove to Nuha's house. It was a huge three-story building. Tt looked like a mansion with a big fountain in the front and a security gate.

We rang the door, and Nuha came down the long garden and opened the gate. Hatem introduced me to her. They had several dogs that sniffed me. We walked to the house, into the large balcony. Nuha's mom and aunts were there to greet us. We sat down.

Nuha's mom introduced herself as Aya. Could this be the very same person mom asked me to go and see? Amazing enough, she was!

"I'm supposed to look for you and send you our condolences." I said with a shocked look on my face. "My dad and your husband were best friends." She said that she knew my dad but had never met my mom and my two brothers.

We sat down and had a soda. They offered me a beer. I said, "No thank you. I don't drink." If she had asked me that question a few years earlier, she would have gotten a different answer, but I was now, thankfully, a new man!

She insisted that I stay till dinner. (Dinner is normally served around 3 PM.) I agreed since I knew that Hatem wasn't about to leave anytime soon. I started talking to Nuha's aunts about America, and how great America is. They remembered my dad and told me a few stories about him when he was young.

They talked about the Jewelry store he owned in the downtown area and how he always dressed in expensive suits. They told me about my grandma who had great faith. They told me that she used to enter her room, close the door, and pray in the nude. She prayed and prayed for my dad and his kids. Wow. My grandma was a believer and she prayed for me! That meant so much to me. I had a nightmare or two over the "praying in the nude" part, but I assume it was too hot to pray with clothes on!

We ate dinner and I had to do what I always do, till this day: I had to take a power nap. I reclined back on one of the chairs in their balcony and took a nap. Hatem did the same. I felt so comfortable around these strangers to the point that I could go to sleep at their home.

Twenty minutes later, a beautiful young lady walked into the house. She had light brown hair, green eyes, and very light skin. She looked European. She was Nuha's sister.

What a contrast! Nuha had black hair and brown eyes. I woke up and looked at her. She didn't see me at first. She kissed her aunts and they prepared her dinner. She worked at the Arab bank in Gaza and had just came home from work. Hatem introduced me to her. She said, that she met all my cousins but didn't know I existed.

I was watching her politely. She looked different. Her voice has a scratch to it and sounded beautiful. She asked me if I smoked, I said, "No I don't smoke." Her mom told her I didn't drink alcohol either.

She didn't give me much attention. She looked at Hatem and told him that she had four tickets to a concert that night at the YMCA. A Swedish band was performing there.

Maha said that Hatem, Nuha, and her should go. Hatem asked, "What about the extra ticket? Can Nazareth come with us? She said, "That's fine."

An hour later, we drove to the concert. Maha and I sat in the back and didn't talk much. We arrived at the concert and there were thousands of people. It was very loud. Gaza is the highest populated place on Earth. Unemployment is very high. Most the population are under the age of 20. I think the majority of them were at the concert that night.

Maha and I didn't talk much at the concert. They were very impressed with the entertainment, but as for me, I'd seen Michael Jackson, Tina Turner, Guns N Roses, Kenny Rogers, and many others in concert. I had turned into a spoiled American.

Nuha suggested we go to a local restaurant afterwards, so we did. At dinner, I was trying to find an opportunity to share Christ with them. I knew my cousin Hatem was an Atheist, but I didn't care. I loved him, and I knew he was a lazy Atheist. He didn't do his homework to see if there was a God or not.

Once the food got there, Hatem asked me why I look so happy. I told him and the girls that I was a Christian and that God changed my life. I said: "That before knowing Jesus, I was like an old car that kept breaking down, but now that I was a Christian, I was that same old car, but it felt like I was married to a mechanic, and I had AAA on speed dial."

Hatem was visibly upset, looked at the girls and said, "Don't listen to him. He's a Born Again Christian."

To my shock, Maha, Nuha's sister said: "Me, too."

It felt like a lighting hit me. I started shaking, and I hit the table so hard with both arms. The drinks splashed and some of the plates fell to the ground. *WHAT? REALLY?* I felt that God was prompting me to say what I said next. I looked at her and said, "Would you like to marry me?" She was the one! The one I prayed for the last three years.

I knew I couldn't afford to get married. I wasn't planning to get married. I came to Gaza to finish some paperwork and leave. Really God? Did you bring me all the way to this part of the world to meet the woman I was praying for? I thought to myself. "I thought you would bring her to me in Newport Beach, in Irvine, not Gaza!"

She looked at me and said, "I've been praying for a believer to come to this side of the world. Someone who is serious about his walk with God. Not a Christian by name. I will take you seriously. I will pray and fast for three days and will get back to you."

I said, "That's great." I then took her sister Nuha aside and bombarded her with questions about Maha. For a beautiful woman like that in Gaza, Maha should've been married by now. She was 24 years of age at the time. She had so many qualified bachelors ask for her hand in marriage, but she refused because her first criteria was: 'The one I marry has to be a serious Christian. Someone who loves God and walks with Him.'

Maha told me later, that she noticed something different about me. I didn't drink or smoke. That night, Maha invited me to a small home Bible study at one of her friend's home. I said, a "A Bible Study in Gaza? *Really?*"

Yes.

The next day we both went to the Bible study. I met some serious believers who suffered persecution in various ways in Gaza.

Gaza wasn't as bad as it got later, under the Hamas leadership, but Gaza is not as secular as other places like the West Bank or Jordan.

We worshiped God in Arabic. My Arabic was bad. I haven't spoken in Arabic very much in the United Sates. I was rusty. The first three years in Ohio, I hardly spoke any Arabic. When my dad and mom arrived in the U.S., I refused to speak to them in Arabic. I wanted them to learn the language. Even when my dad talked to me in Arabic, I responded in English.

Maha and some of her friends were laughing at my funny Arabic. That was okay, I was a Comedian. A laugh's a laugh, right? But we worshiped and prayed together. I spent the next two days going back and forth to the courthouse to finish the deed for my dad's portion of the house that he owned with the rest of the family.

On the third day, I was invited to Aya's home for dinner. She is now Maha's mom to me. I still can't believe how God wanted to make sure I got to that house. Even if Hatem didn't bring me there, I was supposed to go there and meet Maha.

Right after I got there, Maha arrived from work. The dinner table was ready. It was a great feast. I looked at Maha and said cautiously, "It is the third day of your fasting. Are you still praying and fasting?" She smiled and said, "I'm starving. Let's do it!"

I can never forget these words. She said yes! I was single, but now I was preparing to get married. Hope in 24 hours. We started planning the engagement party. I rushed with my other cousin to the Jewelry District (the Caesarea), to buy the ring.

Something shocking happened to me when I started entering the Caesarea. One old man stopped me and said curiously: "Is your dad Hanna Rizkallah?" I said, "Yes. How did you know?"

He said, "Your dad used to own one of the stores here. Let me walk you there to see it." I asked him how he knew I was Hanna's son. My dad has been gone from Gaza for over 30 years.

He explained that I looked like him when he was young. We walked into the store that my dad used to own. I looked around. I was filled with nostalgic feelings.

I ended up buying her ring from the same store my dad owned 30 year earlier.

We spent the next few days planning the engagement. Maha worked at a bank and I went there few times around lunch time to see her. I had to be very careful about the cultural taboos. I couldn't be alone with Maha at any time. When we went out, her sister or her cousin's son came along for the ride. Remember that scene in "The Godfather" when Michael and his fiancé were walking along and were followed by her entire family? It was like that times about ten.

We had a great time at my cousin's wedding. I was the best man. The next day, I swam in the Mediterranean. That was a great experience. Maha and I spent every day together. We then had our engagement party. I asked my uncle and few other elders from my family to come with me and ask for Maha's hand. Her dad had passed on, but her uncle Elias was the one that represented her side of the family.

I remember her mom saying this to me: "I normally grill anyone who comes to ask for one of my daughters in marriage, with so many questions, but you are different. Maha had so many eligible bachelors, from Doctors to Engineers to Business men ask for her hand but she refused.

She wanted to marry a Christian Believer. Her aunts told her, and I believed them, that she would never get married, that she would end up like them, old and single." She added, "So, I believe that God brought you here to Gaza to marry my daughter.

Therefore, I will not interfere with what God is doing."

She then asked me what I do for a living? I told her that I was a Comedian. I do Accounting, but I'm a Comedian. She said, and I'll never forget what she said, "What if they don't laugh, how are you going to pay the bills?" I didn't have an answer for her. She wasn't expecting one either.

We had a beautiful engagement party. Maha was wearing a hot pink dress and looked like a doll. I presented her with the gold necklace, bracelet, and ring that I bought for her from my dad's old place. We danced a little and then went together for a ride in the car alone. We drove by the seashore. We parked the car and talked. We then prayed together. It was so beautiful to pray together.

We had our first kiss there. Right on the shores of the Mediterranean. The smell of roasted chestnuts and corn on the cob filled the air. The sky was so clear and bright stars filled the dark sky. We prayed together a little longer. We then drove back to her home, and I started getting ready to leave. I had to come back to the States.

1995- 1996

Maha and I spent an entire year apart. We spent countless hours courting over the phone. I don't know who benefited directly from my long-distance bills, but some Telephone Executive has comfortably retired on a desert island from my charges alone.

I came home with no money in my savings account. My parents never taught me the value of money. My dad was very generous and that is one of the great things I got from him. I love to give and help. I didn't know how to save money. So, one of the things I did to help me save for the wedding, was to open a bank account at a bank that was far enough from my home so that I couldn't access the money quickly.

What I did next was to commit to putting every extra dollar that I earned into the bank. When a church gave me a love offering, which most times there was little to no love in the offering, I would take that money, drive to the ATM machine at that bank and deposit it.

I prayed and asked God to provide the money needed for my marriage.

At the time, Northwest Airlines and Sprint had a deal. For every dollar I spent on my phone bill, I would get air miles.

I called Maha every night. She was ten hours ahead of me. I think to this day that she is ten hours ahead of me. She asks me to take the trash out and ten hours later I do it. I think every woman is ten hours ahead of her husband.

I looked forward to these calls. I would get home; shut my room door; call Maha and talk and talk and talk. We talked about life, our future, having kids . . . etc. We prayed together. We still wrote letters to each other.

I think courting over the phone was better than dating. For example, if we were courting at the same place, when you go to a restaurant with your fiancé or date, you spend time looking for parking, picking a restaurant, looking at the menu, choosing the food you want, getting distracted with the surroundings. We didn't have to worry about any of that over the phone.

Gaza, where Maha lived, is a third world country. They don't have all the luxuries we have here in America. They don't have the latest fashions, especially when it comes to shopping for a wedding. What I did that I'm proud of, is that I bought two copies of a Bridal magazine. It was about 200 pages and it had everything; wedding dresses, wedding cakes, everything that had to do with weddings. I sent a copy to Maha. I kept the other one, so we could both be on the same page.

Once she got it, she picked a dress. She asked me to turn to a certain page and look at it. She picked the wedding glasses, the ornaments, the stuff you put on the wedding cake. All I had to do was find the page, mark it, and order it.

One thing Maha and I agreed to: My life began when I accepted Christ. When I turned my life over to God I became a new man. We didn't discuss my bad decisions and immoral life style before that. I was a new creation. I know it's a stretch, but I became a Born-Again Virgin. I kept myself pure from that moment on. And that became my new past. I respected Maha for agreeing with me and for committing to that.

I was counting the days until I could go back and see her. It had been almost a year. When I went back for the wedding, my luggage was full of wedding stuff. I also carried the wedding dress with me on the plane. The flight attendants were very kind to make sure it was kept in a safe place on the plane.

I worked hard that year. I saved the money needed for the wedding. We also decided to do our honeymoon in Greece. Greece was very close to Israel, and I was able to book a cruise.

God provided the money. I saved $25,000 that year. That was more than I was making. God took care of it. Some churches gave me more money than what I asked for. Calls were coming in for gigs.

At the time, my middle brother, Emad, and I rented a town-home in Newport Beach. It was in the poor section of Newport

Beach. I called it: "Newpoor Beach". Well, we were actually in Costa Mesa, CA, but the zoning had us in Newport Beach. My mom lived with us. My mom has always lived with me since she left Kuwait. The only time we were separated was the first 2 years of college.

Mom and Emad decided to attend the wedding. Emad had left Kuwait and moved to the U.S. in 1989. He studied engineering in Detroit and moved back to Kuwait to work. In 1989, he decided to move in with us. At the time, we lived in Garden Grove, CA. I rented a small house there. Emad started working at the same Subway where I worked. He was a Civil Engineer making sandwiches, cleaning the restaurant, and working minimum wage . . . but that's how you start.

I always tell people who arrive to America, this is the land of opportunity. You will make it here if you are willing to work hard. There are no short cuts. You must pay your dues, and you must pay the price. The great thing about America is that no one can stop you while you're climbing the ladder of success. No one will stop you because of your background, race, religion, or whatever family you come from. It may seem commonplace to you, but to a man like me, it's a Country sent from Heaven!

In other countries, you might not be allowed to hold certain jobs because of your race or background. When I lived in Kuwait, I worked for a bank for a short period of time. There were certain jobs that were reserved for native Kuwaitis only. I couldn't apply for or get them regardless of how smart I was or how hard I was willing to work. In some Countries, there are certain neighborhoods you cannot live in unless your family was wealthy or had a good reputation. But not in America. If you can afford it, you can live anywhere you want!

The CEO of a company and the Janitor can go to the same restaurant for lunch, they can shop at the same mall and both can carry the same brand of cell phone.

Americans don't care about your last name. When you lived in Kuwait, the name of your family influenced the way people treated you.

Most of the immigrants I know worked hard and made it. A lot of them love to work at or own a Convenient store or a Gas Station. You can work 24 hours a day if you want to at these businesses. There is no shame in working. America teaches you that. The Middle Eastern mentality was different. There, people don't want to be a Janitor, a Bus Boy, a Dish-washer or a Maid.

But in America there is dignity in every job. The immigrants that came to this Country and felt entitled to everything this Country offers without being willing to pay the price, ended up moving back to their home Countries.

Emad worked hard and eventually did an internship at California Department of Transportation. He worked for free for an entire year. I encouraged him to stay at it. He worked there in the morning and in the evening and on weekends, he worked at Subway. Eventually it paid off. A year later he was hired as a Civil Engineer and, to this day, he is still working for them.

Since Emad couldn't go back after Saddam Hussain invaded the Kuwait, he applied for asylum and was granted that. Therefore, it was very difficult for him to leave the U.S. and attend the wedding. But he did. He and Mom flew to Egypt and entered Gaza thru the Rafah Border. Emad was my best man at the wedding.

The trip back was a stark contrast from the first trip I took. This time I was the happiest passenger on that KLM flight from

Los Angeles to Ben Gurion Airport in Israel. Holding a wedding dress didn't make it any easier going through the interrogations. The drive from Ben Gurion to the Eritz Border didn't seem long at all. I made it through and took a taxi to Maha's home. It was just like the movies. I rang the bell to her house, and she ran down the stairs, through the garden, and opened the gate. She jumped on me and hugged me. We forgot we were in Gaza. We could've been arrested!

We spent almost every minute together. We hand-delivered most of the wedding invitations. You don't need to give much notice to people in Gaza. They are ready to attend a wedding even if they get invited that same day. It was their only outlet to dance and have a good time.

We had our wedding at the YMCA building in Gaza. Over 600 people attended the ceremony. We got married the Greek Orthodox way. Neither Maha nor I were ready to wage a family and social war by getting married at a Protestant Church. Immediately after we arrived in the States, we had my friend, Pastor Steve Hurley, officiate a small wedding at the Church on Redhill where I was attending.

Maha looked so pretty coming down the aisle. Since her dad was deceased, her uncle, Elias, walked the aisle with her. I was standing there looking at her and thanking God for answering my prayers.

Our Greek Orthodox wedding was long. We had to go in circles several times; There was incense and lots of kissing. Not each other, but kissing the cross, the Bible, and other iconic items and hands that Maha and I refused to do. It all sounded Greek to us, but we went through it, with my brother, and best man next to me with a 104 degree Fahrenheit fever.

Following the wedding ceremony, I stood next to the rest of the wedding party and shook hands with 600 people. Most had to introduce themselves and tell me how they were related to me or Maha. I was three when I left the Holy Land, so I had no memory of who was who.

A few hours later we headed to the Palestine Hotel, the biggest hotel in Gaza at the time, and had the reception. Maha and I insisted on no-alcohol served at the wedding.

An hour into the wedding, the air-conditioning stopped. It was August in Gaza. Translation: hot and humid. I went to the manager to inquire. He said that the electricity at his hotel could not handle both lights and air-conditioning at the same time.

I said, "Where you aware of this problem when we signed the contract?"

He said, "Yes, but it never came up."

"What do you mean it never came up?" I replied, "I thought the banquet room came with lights and air-conditioning?"

"Well, choose one." He said authoritatively. "Either lights or air."

That is where the Arabic culture comes clashing with the American culture in meaning what you say. In America when you say, "I will do this today," it means today. In the Middle East it might mean today, tomorrow, or in few days within the week.

The number 4 to an American means Four. In the Middle East it may mean 3, 4 or 5. Nobody is lying or not keeping their end of the deal. It just means what it means to the person making the promise.

God bless America. If this thing happened, the hotel would have a reputation to keep. You can ask for a refund, go to Yelp and complain, or call the Hotel's Corporate office. Not in Gaza. You don't have that privilege.

Eventually, we opened the windows and kept the lights.

Maha and I danced and talked to each other all night. We weren't aware of the rest of the guests. We were in our own world. Towards the end of the wedding, people started coming up to the stage area where Maha and I were seated. They shook my hand, opened a box of jewelry, and put the jewelry on Maha. That was the cultural thing of giving wedding gifts. There were a line of people waiting to do the same thing. I was so happy to see that. Some gave Maha rings, bracelets, and necklaces.

By the time they were all done, I was laughing at Maha because she looked like Snoop Dog, the rapper. She had several gold chains, gold rings, and bracelets on.

These gifts were all sold few years later to make up for the small income we were living from in the Comedy business.

Following the wedding, we flew to Greece from Tel Aviv and spent a few days on a cruise ship touring the Greek Isles. We also spent a day in Ephesus, Turkey where Paul the Apostle spent some time. Then my brother Ramzi and his wife joined us in Santorini, Greece for few days since they couldn't attend the wedding.

Santorini to me was Heaven on Earth. I loved being with Maha after spending a year talking on the phone. We were together at last.

What amazes me about how I met Maha is that one day I was single. 24 hours later—after her three days of fasting and praying—I was planning a wedding. I waited on the Lord and prayed, and God blessed me. I remember after I came to know Christ, I would go to the Balboa Peninsula where Yamo lived with his two young boys, and would spend hours sitting on the beach at night, listening to the waves crashing and praying to God, asking Him to bless me with a beautiful Godly wife and to bless my career and in due time to bless me with children. I prayed to become a full-time Comedian in the Christian market.

God answered my prayers. I'm married to the beautiful Godly woman I prayed for. Eventually He provided the money and the rest. Believe me, I never take anything for granted. Except when the air conditioning goes out. No one should have to tolerate that!

CHAPTER 7
SEVERANCE PAY IS OK!

The Third Hope in 24 Hours

It was a memorable day when I went in to work.

I worked for Restaurant Enterprises Group, Inc., the Irvine parent company of such eateries as Coco's, Carrows, and El Torito restaurants.

I'd been juggling Comedy and Accounting at the same time. I thought of myself as a Comedian having a day job. My goal and prayer were to become a full-time Comedian.

But since I left Hollywood and transitioned to the new Christian market, I didn't know how I could possibly survive doing Comedy full time.

I was one of a few Comedians who was doing this specifically for the Christian market. Chonda Pierce, Mark Lowry, Mike

Warneke, Robert G. Lee, Mike Williams, and Paul Aldrich were mostly the only ones working that market.

Later on, Thor Ramsey, Brad Stine, Jeff Allen, Michael Jr. and a few other club Comedians jumped into the Christian's market scene.

I was a go-getter. When I turned my life to Christ and got the call to start doing comedy to honor God, I didn't wait for the phone to ring. I didn't know what else to do, so I started calling churches. Some Church Pastors called me the devil. I would hear them sputter out, "How can you attempt to bring a worldly thing such as comedy to the church?" for about a second before I heard the click. . . . and the phone hung up.

The market was very small, but my church on Redhill, and Pastor Randy were ahead of their time. We started a Comedy Club at the church called The Christian Comedy Club. We had T-shirts made and had volunteers serving as waiters and staff. I booked a Comedian once a month. That's when I met one of the funniest and creative Comedians in the television warm-up and film industry; Robert G. Lee who, 20 years later, became my comedy buddy. That means we get together and write comedy together.

Although I was attending the Church on Redhill, a Southern Baptist church, I was listening to a radio station called KWAVE. I listened to it daily for teaching. I listened to Pastor Chuck Smith from the Calvary movement. I also listened to Pastor Greg Laurie who used a lot of comedy in his teachings. He was an Evangelist. I also listened to Pastors such as David Rosales, Raul Ries, and a few others. I was so hungry for the Word of God. A few years later, I would join these Pastors on stage at various Men's Conferences.

That day when I got to work, I was called to the Comptroller's office. According to Wikipedia, a Comptroller is a "management level position responsible for supervising the quality of accounting and financial reporting of an organization." Yeah, I don't know what it means either. But I knew the person in that office had authority over me.

The Comptroller was a nice guy. Many times, I stopped by his office and shared the latest joke I heard or made up. I was his relief time away from all the meetings and serious atmosphere accounting offered.

He liked me because I was funny and was The Employee of the Month several times. That day he looked pale. He wasn't smiling. He asked me to come in into his large office and closed the door.

My heart dropped. What did I do wrong? Did I forget to file a return and now the IRS was hitting our company with a hefty penalty? Or worse, was my happy hour half-price appetizer card to El Torito being revoked?

He said: "Nazareth, I know you are one of our best employees and you've been with us for almost 9 years. You are also one of the highest paid staff in your department."

I said, "Yes," waiting for the other shoe to drop. And drop it did.

He said, "Upper Management..."

Upper Management are the people no one knows so everyone can blame them for all the bad decisions the company makes. Though I never actually met anyone from that end of the pay scale, I'm pretty sure Upper Management are people in black robes in a dark dungeon behind the storage room where they sit and make evil decisions.

He continued, and words were coming out of his mouth as if he didn't want to say them. "Upper management decided to lay you off. They wanted to cut the budget in the department and your job is the only one they decided to eliminate." He said apologetically. "I'm so sorry, Nazareth. It will not be the same without you. But I want you to know that they decided to give you six months of severance pay."

"Severance pay! What's that?" I asked.

He said, "That means we will pay you for the next six months as you look for another job."

I got so excited I stood up. With excitement in my voice, I said, "You mean you guys will pay me my regular salary for the next six months while I'm not showing up to work?"

He said, "Nazareth, please don't be sarcastic. This is hurting me more that it is hurting you."

I said, "I'm not being sarcastic. See, you don't understand. I've been praying to God to make me a full-time Comedian, but I didn't know how it was going to happen. These six months of pay can ease the transition. Thank you, God."

The Comptroller, to this day, probably thinks I was being sarcastic.

I was not. I was excited. I signed the deal, went to my cubical and collected my stuff. It was difficult. I looked happy, so my co-workers didn't think anything bad had happened. The truth is, it took all of my willpower to not tap dance out of there!

I went home that day and while driving home I was thinking of how to tell my new bride that I was laid off. I wasn't sure how to put a positive spin on the fact that we might not have an income in six months. I didn't want to tell her what I told the Comptroller that morning. I didn't tell her that this was what I really wanted to do. It felt as it was too soon. I knew most women have a strong need for security and feel insecure when there is no money coming in.

I got home and immediately called my wife to the bedroom. At the time, my mother and my brother lived with us in the same 3-bedroom town-house. We didn't have privacy except in the bedroom where we could talk. Maha followed me to the bedroom and closed the door.

"What's wrong Honey?" she asked.

I said, "I lost my job today. I was laid off. But with my credentials I'm sure I can get a job tomorrow. Now, don't you worry about anything. They gave me six-month's worth of salary, and if I find a job quickly we could have a double salary for few months; one from the new job and one from the severance pay."

She didn't ask me why I was fired. She didn't get flustered in the least. My new bride said, "You know what Honey? I know you love to do Comedy. I know God called you to do Comedy. I know that it will make you happier. Why don't you go for it?"

I tried to hide my excitement and wanted to make her aware of her decision. I said, "But Honey if I do that, we might starve for the next 10 years." (and we did)

She replied, "I would rather have a happy, broke husband than a miserable Accountant with money."

I said, "Are you sure?"

She said, with her typical faith comforting tone, "God will take care of us. He will not leave us." Oh, that statement was repeated so many times by Maha so many times over the next 10 years.

I was so excited. I hugged her. We prayed together and asked God to bless my career.

What a day. Whether the world cared or not, I was now a full-time Christian Comedian. This was exactly what I wanted. I couldn't quit on my own, but God was so kind to me. He did it for me. That's right, I'm giving God credit for firing me. He also put peace in my bride's heart to accept His calling for me to be a full-time Comedian. From that day to this, I've not had a "regular" job.

Hope in 24 hours. One day, I was an employee in a Tax-Accounting company, the next day, I was a full-time Comedian!

One day, I'm waiting and praying. The next day: God answers.

God bless America that a person can do what he or she loves <u>and</u> get paid for it.

That day, I had that extra love and respect for Maha for her willingness to sacrifice so much, to allow me to do what I love to do. I never forgot that, and I never will. When I say we went through ten long, lean years after that decision, you'd better believe it!

I'm a fortunate man to be married to a wonderful woman who is selfless. Her wonderful attitude about life and faith makes me want to be selfless as well. The ripple effects are amazing.

I think one of the best glues that can keep a marriage together is selflessness. Thinking of the other partner more than yourself. Caring more about them than yourself. That is the best advice I can give to a married couple.

Also, praying together. I pray with Maha. But another advice I jokingly pray is this, "Lord thank you for giving me a forgetful wife. Whatever stupid things I say and do, she forgets about them as far as the East is from the West. And for that, I'm so thankful!"

She then jokingly prays, "Lord, thank You for Nazareth. I know you love him so much, you want him to be in Your presence. Please use me as a vessel to accomplish Thy Will Oh Lord."

God always, always, always came through for us.

The Gold Watch

Our first ten years of Comedy after I was laid off my accounting job, were filled with many weeks of having no money. Naturally, since we were broke, God decided to bless us with more responsibility to test our faith. In 1998, we had our first child John.

When John was born, I was a full-time Comedian working the church market. If nothing else, I was diligent. I was making 50 cold calls a day. Almost all of these calls were returned with rejections.

I served as the President of the Christian Comedy Association for almost three years. The CCA was formed when several Christian Comedians decided they needed to have a gathering where they could meet for fellowship, pray and learn together. By that time almost 30 Comedians were serving in the Faith-Based market. The majority of us got together at Chonda Pierce's Funny Farm in Nashville. Chonda Pierce served for few months as the 2nd President of the Association following Dan Rupple, from Isaac Airfreight Improv Group, who was our first President. I took over from Chonda.

During one of the conferences we had, I was asked by other Comedians why I'm considered one of the hardest working Comedians in the business. They wondered how I got a lot of bookings. I responded with, "I'm the one who gets most of the rejections. If you are willing to call and ask for shows and are willing to be rejected, sooner or later, they will say 'Yes' and hire you."

I did get a lot of rejections, but I kept calling and asking. I needed to take care of my family. I needed to make money. I was writing constantly, reading comedy books as well. With a new baby, it wasn't easy.

We hardly had money to pay for diapers. We never wanted to use Food Stamps. Again, I'm not against people using Food Stamps, but it wasn't for me. I came to this country to contribute not to use the system, even in times of need.

I remember walking the aisles at grocery stores praying that I could find a box of diapers with the outside of the box damaged, or even opened so that they could sell it to us for half-price.

To afford the expense of buying John clothes, Maha got a seasonal job at Baby Gap. It was difficult, but we made ends meet. There were a few Pastors that sensed our need and gave me a good honorarium. Others insisted on giving a love offering. But it was exciting to not know how much I'd be making after the show. Maha would be waiting for my call, right after the show, to tell her how much I'd made that night. When I didn't call, she knew it was much less than expected. Some Pastors would thoughtlessly tell me that it would take them a week or so to count the offering and send me a check. At that stage of our life, every dollar that came our way needed to come ASAP. The bills and the rent couldn't wait.

One time, one of my wealthy relatives came to visit us. He stayed with us for few weeks. As he left back to the airport, he told me that he was aware of our financial situation and he wanted to help. He then proceeded to take his gold watch off his wrist and handed it to me. He said, "Nazareth, this is a very expensive watch. I want to give it to you. If you need money, you can sell it and make a lot of money!"

I was excited. This is the first time someone gave me something that I didn't work for. I always worked for everything I had. I couldn't wait to go home and tell Maha.

Maha was not very excited about the handout. She just reminded me to trust God.

For me, I had a little more peace knowing that if push came to shove and I couldn't pay the rent on time, I would go sell the watch and pay the rent for many months.

We always paid our rent the last day of the grace period. We struggled, but we paid it. It was several months later, that the last day of the grace period arrived and we didn't have the money. The mail came in, and there were no checks in the mail. I didn't know what to do. Maha always seemed calmer about finances than me. It was hard to shake her faith. She always reminded me to trust God.

I ran to the bedroom, went into one of the drawers, grabbed the watch, took it out of the box I had it in, and went downstairs and told Maha that today was the day. We were going to sell the watch!

She was reluctant, but we had no other option. We need to drop off the money to the landlord that evening.

We drove to a Jeweler on 17th Street in Costa Mesa, CA, right by the old Mother's Market. I went in and told the Jeweler that I was ready to sell this expensive watch. He looked at it and asked me if he could open the back cover and look at the inside of the watch. I agreed. A few minutes later, he asked me if he could have his co-worker look at it as well and give his opinion? I agreed as long as the watch stayed in my view. His friend came out of the back and started examining the watch. After few minutes, the Jeweler looked at me and said, "I can give you $17.00 for that watch!" I was shocked. I said, you mean $17,000, right? He said, "No, $17.00. This watch is made in China. It is a fake watch." I said, "But what about the gold?" He said, "That is not gold." I was in shock. Not only was I just as broke as when the day started, but my rich relative was a liar! I took the watch and walked out to my car where Maha was waiting for me. She saw the sadness in my eyes.

She guessed the problem immediately. She said, "Was it a fake watch?"

I said, "Yes, it's made in China!"

She said, "Wow, and you put your hope in it instead of God."

I said, "Don't rub it in honey. How can we pay the rent today?

She said what she always said when I asked her that question, "Trust God!" I said, "How can I trust God when the rent is due today? The mail is already here and there are no checks. How can I trust God?"

She said, "I really don't know, but I know that God will never leave us nor forsake us!"

We were quiet the rest of the way home. A few minutes after we arrived home, there was knocking at the door and it was the FedEx guy. He handed me a package and I signed for it. When I opened the envelope, it was a letter from my ex- employer that explained to me that the 401-K they had for me wasn't moved to a different account in due time, so they are sending me the balance. With the letter was a check for $1425.00. Exactly the amount we needed for rent.

I was screaming with excitement, "Oh Maha. You are right. God will not leave us. We have the rent! We have the rent!"

I ran to the bank, put the check in the account, drove to the landlord and gave him the rent check.

Afterwards, I was so ashamed of myself for trusting in a watch and not in the God of the Universe. Sometimes we forget that God knows what we need before we ask Him for it. He cares about the details of our life.

God always came through for us. I sometimes get frustrated and say, "Why God? Why do you have to wait till the last minute to rescue us?"

I guess He was strengthening my faith.

I'm a graduate of the University of Financial faith. I trust God completely with finances. God now uses me to encourage others who are going through financial hardships. It may not be the main reason God had us go through such hard times, but personally I think that's a huge part of the puzzle.

With this hard-earned empathy, Maha and I can feel for others in need and many times we have been privileged to help families and individuals. Because of what we went through, it's never lost on us what it feels like to be short of covering your basic needs.

One time, back in 2008, when the economy took a dive in the U.S., performers were having a hard time finding work. Most corporations stopped hiring entertainment, churches were laying off Pastors and would never consider hiring Entertainers. We struggled, but God saw us through. I resorted to teaching Comedy Classes to make ends meet. That was one thing I knew I could do; I could teach people how to become Comedians or Humorous Speakers.

During this dark period, I met with a friend who is a great Magician. Chris was struggling financially. His home had just gone through a foreclosure, and he wasn't getting a lot of gigs. We decided to meet at a local restaurant in Santa Ana and pray together. When we arrived there, we ordered the special. It was the cheapest thing on the menu; the Cornish Hen with mashed potatoes.

I then proceeded to share stories with Chris of how God had come through for us financially; how He took care of every need we had. I told him of the story of the watch and how Chris needed to put his trust in God. I then asked him to bow his head and pray with me.

At that time, the waiter came and quietly brought our orders. I was deep into praying. I got to the verse in the Book of Matthew, chapter 6 in the Holy Bible that said that God takes care of the little birds and how much more important are we than that the little birds. Right then, I opened one eye and looked at my plate, and there was a little bird in my plate cooked to perfection. I stopped then continued with: "Except for that one Lord!"

I never doubted God's Word, but that day was the closest I came to it!

Youth Events

In my Bible, I keep a few pieces of paper with a hole in the middle of them that have the word "Dad" written on them. I collected them few years ago, while I was teaching a week long High School Camp in Northern Pennsylvania. On the last day of the camp, I was teaching on forgiveness, and I asked the students to write down the name of a person that they hate on a small piece of paper. I told them to think of a person that they have a hard time forgiving and that after they fill in the name, they should bring that paper to the front of the room, where there was a wooden cross, nails, and a few hammers. I asked the students to nail that piece of paper to the cross and go back to their seat and pray and ask God to help them forgive that person.

When the session was over, all the students and Youth Pastor left the room to go to the Cafeteria. I stayed back and collected the pieces of paper. To my shock over 90% of the papers had the word "Dad" written on them. I froze, I knelt to the ground and asked God that my children would never have to ask Him to help them forgive me.

It was a rainy morning in Southern California. My wife tucked the kids all bundled up in their pajamas in the back seat of the car, and they dropped me off at the Ontario Airport. I was heading to Tampa, FL with a connection in Phoenix.

As usual I sat in my exit seat since I couldn't get an upgrade to first class. That's a fringe benefit of frequent travel. A few seconds before closing the plane door, a young 16-year-old African American girl, I'll call her Sandy, struggled her way to the seat next to me and asked if it was taken.

I politely said no, but since she was under 18 years of age, the rules clearly state she couldn't sit in an exit seat anyway because the flight attendant would have to reseat her.

Since it was none of my business I kept my mouth shut. More times than I can count, I speak when it is not appropriate and when it is none of my business. I don't work for the airlines. They don't pay me to enforce the rules. She started to cry and to explain what a horrible day she had already, and it was only 9 AM. I apologized, got up and helped her with her carry on and helped her settle in the exit seat next to me.

Luckily for her, the Flight Attendant didn't ask her age and the plane started to taxi down the runway.

Sandy opened her carry-on luggage and started to panic. "Oh no, I forgot something, I need to go back." Again, I couldn't keep my mouth shut, I asked her what it was, and she said she forgot her mother's ashes. "Oh no", I said. "Did she just die? Were you here in California for the funeral?" She said, "No, she died back in July in Las Vegas and this was my only chance to come back to California to pick up her ashes."

"I'm sorry," I replied. "Where is your father?" She said she hadn't seen her father since she was five years old, and that her father had 22 children and her mother had 6 children! She lived with a guardian now since she couldn't live with her father because he did something to her and the State would not allow her to be near him.

Oh, my heart was broken for that little girl. "How horrible can life get? She's only 16 and she had been through a lot of relocating." I said to myself.

I looked at her, with my Bible open, and said to her: "Honey, Jesus Christ can be a Father to you. He loves you so much. He knows what you've been through and He came to earth to save us from the very sin that caused your life to be miserable." She told me that she went to church a few times in the past and that her new guardian wanted to take her to church every Sunday.

God Bless America for people who act like guardians, foster parents, and those who adopt children.

I pulled out a few of the papers from the Youth Conference I did in Northern Pennsylvania and showed them to Sandy. She asked what they were, and I shared the story with her. She began to cry. I asked if I could pray for her and she bowed her head and we prayed. Sandy began to tell me that she wanted to be a good role model to kids who were her age and I encouraged her to walk close to Christ and serve Him.

She looked like a new person after that prayer. She actually started to smile. I still don't know if she ever got her mom's ashes, but I hope she gets to see her some day on the other side.

To my readers who are reading this, keep in mind there are young people out there that are hurting. They have been through a great amount of pain already. They need us to encourage them, let them know that there is still good out there in the world. Let us not focus on what they *shouldn't* be doing. There is a time and place for that down the road. The most important thing you can do is to give grace. It's what Jesus did, so I don't see any reason why we shouldn't imitate our true Father.

One event I did that same year really changed the way I looked at my audience. I was performing at a Youth Rally at a Church in Fontana, CA. After an hour of Comedy, I presented the Gospel and did the invitation.

Out of a group of over a hundred, only two people came forward to receive Christ. That's a bad batting average. "What's going on Lord? I'm used to a larger percentage than that." I said to myself. "What's going on? Is Wall Street in Heaven having a bad day?"

"Did I not convince them enough with the invitation?" I thought to myself. "Should I go for a second invitation?"

Only two people. One is enough to prime the party in Heaven, since the Bible tells us that if one person comes to Christ, the angels in Heaven rejoice. "But, God? I'm used to more." I looked back at the Worship Leader playing the guitar and asked him to stretch the 'Come Just as You Are' song. Repeat it! Do something. I finally had to go to the "What if tonight was your last night on this earth? Are you ready to meet Jesus?" Nobody else got up of his or her seat. So, I had no choice but to go to the closing prayer to receive Jesus for the sake of these two teenagers.

They were twins, about 17 years of age, and spoke broken English. I prayed a prayer and they repeated it after me.

I went home that night, not very pleased with the results.

I received a phone call the next morning. It was the Youth Pastor from the church. He didn't sound all right.

I said, "What's wrong Mike?

He said, "Remember the two teenagers that came forward last night after the invitation?"

I said, "Yes. I do remember. Rub it in. I know there were only two."

He said, "They're from Thailand. They just came in to the U.S. to stay with their aunt few days ago. Somebody invited them to our church."

He continued, "After you left last night, they went home. They had a bike. One rode on the bike and the other rode in the basket in front of it. Five minutes later an incoming car hit them. One of the twins died on the spot. The other is in intensive care."

Pastor Mike told me that while he was visiting the surviving teenager in the hospital, the teen's aunt brought a Buddha statue to put in his room for good luck, but the teenager told her. "I don't need that! I'm a Christian. I believe in Jesus Christ."

WOW. God waited for them to give them an opportunity to accept Him. What a wonderful God!

People need hope. People need Jesus. You need Jesus. You need encouragement. Maybe you're still alive because God is waiting for you to accept Him and receive that gift that He is offering you . . . the Gift of Eternal Life and the gift of Abundant Life here on this Earth.

How long will you wait to respond to Him? What are you waiting for? What are you putting your hope in? A Gold Watch from China?

CHAPTER 8
I LEASED MY KIDS

A year and a half into our marriage, Maha got pregnant. Some say, "We got pregnant."

I say, "No! She got pregnant. She suffered the nausea, the kicking, and the weight gain."

I just gained weight to sympathize with her. Our stomachs were growing at the same rate, like two cars at a NASCAR race, but you know one of them is going to drop out of the race in 9 months.

During the pregnancy, we started reading every book about childbearing. The book we relied on the most was: "What to Expect When You Are Expecting."

We attended Lamaze classes. I think 'Lamaze' is a French word that means: "Don't worry, the baby is gonna' come out anyway!"

I remember the day our first born, John, was ready to come out. We went walking around the neighborhood in our rented townhouse in Newport Beach. We walked and walked until Maha felt the urge to push, so we hurriedly got back to the house, grabbed the duffle bag and jumped in the car. (Well, Maha didn't jump in the car—she squeezed herself into the passenger seat), and we drove to Hoag hospital.

We got there around 9 PM. ready to exercise what I learned in Lamaze classes.

We knew we were going to name our baby boy, John. John in the Hebrew means *Yochanan,* meaning "YAHWEH is gracious." In the Arabic it is *Hanna.* That was my dad's name, and in our tradition, the oldest boy should name his first-born son after his dad's name. I was the youngest son but neither one of my brothers had kids.

So, I decided to follow the tradition and keep the name.

But since we couldn't call him Hanna, to save him from bullying at school, we called him John.

John had a different agenda that night. He still had more work to do inside his mother's womb, so he wasn't ready to come out until morning. We spent 10 hours in the Maternity Ward trying to get that baby out!

We tried breathing, talking to the baby, and I said stuff like: "Disneyland is only 20 minutes from here. The ice cream truck stops by our home every day."—and many other things to entice John to come out. I knew he was trying, since after he was born, his little nose was bruised from trying to come out naturally.

Finally, the Doctor decided to do a C-Section.

They moved us into the operation room, they dressed me in their nuclear waste protection gear and walked me into the room where my wife was lying there with a little curtain that blocked her from seeing what the Doctor was doing. The curtain was 18 inches wide and 2 inches high. Just enough for her not to see the cut. I was sitting next to her and holding her hand. She said, "I can't see anything?" I answered, "Yes Honey, because we are in the C-Section, next time, we will request the D-Section or the

Balcony and we can see better." She laughed.

Thank God for the epidural. The curtain didn't stop her from smelling the burning flesh smell, and I could see more of my wife that any husband wants to see. But let me state for the record, her internal organs are quite lovely.

The Doctor kept moving organs around trying to get to the placenta. At one point, he actually dropped an organ that dangled from a vein . . . or an artery. I have no idea what it was. Suffice to say, it was not a pretty sight. Then, just when I was about to lose whatever was left in my stomach, he pulled our son out. It was like pulling a cookie from blue and red Jello.

The Attending Nurse took him and washed him, wrapped him up in a tiny blanket, put a little sock on his head and handed him to me.

Oh God. The plethora of emotions that hit you at that moment can't be described. I was a DAD! Just 24 hours ago, I was a husband. Now, 24 hours later, and for the rest of my life, I will have the title, DAD.

I felt responsible. I had to take care of this little thing that I had to provide, protect, and raise. I had baseball mitts to buy and a college to save up for. To say I was overwhelmed would be an understatement.

Then mom said, "Give him to me." I said, "No. He is mine. Get your own."

She cuddled the baby and kissed him while the Surgical Nurse did her seamstress work on my wife. I'm not sure where she learned to sew but she did an OK job. We didn't know Maha was going to have two more C-sections later. If we did, I would've asked her to put a zipper there instead of sewing her backup.

The Nurse then asked me to accompany John to the nursery where they kept babies immediately following birth. The room had 20 brand new, fresh babies. They smelled new. It's like the show room of a car dealership. You look at the baby, then you look at the sticker. Weight, height, etc. I was sure the Hospital Manager was going to come out and ask me, "What's it going to take to get you to take this baby home today?"

They took our precious boy and put him under a heating lamp to keep him warm. It was a better heating lamp that what Denny's restaurant uses. Their food is cold.

My son was enjoying the heat but hated the clean-up process. He held on to my thumb and wouldn't let go. I loved it. He spent the next few hours tightly holding my thumb. I kept asking to go check on Maha but they told me she was still sleeping in the recovery room.

I finally had to do the second hardest thing I've ever done in my life. The first being when I left my dad dying at the hospital and went to do a show. I looked at John and said, "Son, you need to let go. I have to go to a show. Five hundred people are waiting for me in Anaheim to come and make them laugh. I can't cancel it. I will be back in few hours."

I ran to the recovery room, spent few minutes with Maha while she was coming out from under the anesthesia, then ran to the car and drove to the show. I was smiling throughout the entire time. I'll be the first to admit I was on automatic pilot.

I was doing my jokes, but my mind was on that little 7 lbs. 2 oz., 20-inch baby just 20 miles away, not to mention my wife and best friend who was currently recovering from surgery.

I finished my set, got my applause, took my check and drove like a bat out of Hades back to the hospital. If any police had tried to stop me they would have had to chase me all the way to the Recovery Room.

Safely back at the hospital, I had to make the decision: Where do I go first: The Recovery Room or the Nursery? What do you think? The Recovery Room of course!

Before you can appreciate the product, you have to appreciate the factory that produced it. My wife is my own flesh and blood. I ran to her and her first question, like always, was: "How was the show? Did you like it?" It's never, "Did they laugh?" Or, "Did they like you?" She believed in me enough to know the answer to those two questions is always, "*Yes!*"

I kissed her and ran down to see John. He was crying. When he felt my hand, he grabbed my thumb and stopped crying. To this day whenever he's upset I say, "Pull my thumb."

I asked the nurse to bring him to see his mom. She brought him up, handed him to Maha and I sat next to her on the bed praying and thanking God for answering our prayer. We prayed for a healthy baby. Another prayer from the days at the Balboa Beach was answered; to have my own family.

What a blessing it is to have children. Many people do not have that privilege. Some of those attempt the IVF process.

The In Vitro Fertilization process is an expensive procedure. It is the process where they take the eggs from the woman and the wallet from the man, put them together and hope for a baby.

It is natural for us to desire children. Some who cannot afford the IVF try adoption. New adoptive parents can take and care for children from someone else who doesn't want them, can't afford them, or can't be there for them.

I believe adoption is a beautiful thing. I don't know if I can do it yet. Americans are so good at adopting. They have the heart for it.

Whatever way you go about having kids, the end result is you have to raise them. Yikes! All I can say on that subject is that you had better buckle up because it's going to be a bumpy ride!

For the first few months of their life, kids will not be able to walk. They will need devices to move them around. These devices are called Parents . . . with stollers.

Strollers are a pain in the neck. Yes, they have wheels, but those wheels don't help when you're folding it and unfolding it, picking it up and putting it back in the car. Why do they make them that heavy? All you need are wheels, a chair and a basket to put the stuff in. Maybe all you need is a basket with wheels. That would certainly save you money. Moses' mom had the right idea; a floating basket. It never entered my mind before we had John, but I thought the idea was pure genius. Drop the kid at the pier and pick him up at the river next to them all.

Kids cannot walk; also, they're too small to ride in cars without a car seat. I don't care who you are; you'll never be able to install that car seat correctly. Eventually we just used duct tape to hold John in.

Once you have children you start thinking savings. I realized I could no longer spend money like I used to. I had to now save money for the child. If you think I worked hard to raise money for my wedding, having a baby boy pushed me into DefCon 5!

Ladies, do you want to secure a college fund for your baby?

Make your husband pay you one dollar for every time you empty your bladder during pregnancy. Or if you're the father, put a dollar in the jar every time your wife asks you to pull over to get to a restroom. By the ninth month, your baby will be able to afford Harvard.

Sometimes fathers get competitive thoughts in their minds. They think they can understand their baby more than the baby's mother can.

Think again. It's a losing battle for you dads. Wait until the baby is tired or hungry and you'll find out who's their parent of choice.

John wanted to feed constantly. His mom had no choice but breastfeed in public. Breastfeeding is legal in all 50 states. It is not indecent exposure... most shows on HBO are!

Two and a half years after we had John, Carole came along. She was born around Christmas. I wanted to call her Natalie. She was named Natalie for an hour until her aunt, Nuha, called from Baltimore and asked to name her Carole since she was a Christmas Baby.

Although Maha had another C-section to deliver Carole, we both had the attitude of: "Been There Done That." Another healthy baby. Thank you, Lord, for answering our prayers.

Carole immediately became Daddy's Girl. Although she was very unattractive as a baby, she grew to become a gorgeous toddler and today, she is a beauty. People ask me if I'm going to buy a gun to stop the coming onslaught of boys, but I always joke with her and say to her: "Carole, you can date anyone you want as long as they are not allergic to bullets!"

Carole is an intelligent young lady. She's been an "A" student all along, but she wants to attend Harvard Law School. I believe she has a great chance. She's very disciplined.

She also loves God and the Word of God to a point that it keeps boys away from her. They know they have no chance with her. Because of that I sleep much better at night.

After having a boy and a girl, we decided we were done. We were a complete family. We thought about maybe adding a dog or a turtle down the line, but as far as we were concerned, we had done our part to repopulate the earth and didn't feel the need to exceed our limit.

In 2003, we decided to become homeowners. We left our leased townhouse in Newport Beach and bought a small three-bedroom home in Corona, CA. We didn't know why we were moving to Corona, but God Had his own plan in mind.

Corona is on the outskirts of Orange County. It's a 20-minute drive from Disneyland and a 30-minute drive from the beach. All in all, it's a nice middle-class community. There are so many churches in Corona, you forget that you are living in Liberal California. You may or may not know that Orange County is famous for its staunchly Conservative Republican ideals.

Owning a home was weird to me. I never owned a home before and I was not then, nor am I now, "HANDY". I never held a screw driver before. I had no tools and even if I did, I wouldn't know how to use them. So, if you need someone to drive you to the airport or pray for your kids, I'm your man. If you need any help with any repair that is more difficult than screwing in a light bulb, I'd suggest you consult YELP.

We had a small backyard that consisted of two grassy areas separated by an area of small rocks and round pebbles. I decided to save money and buy a used lawnmower, thinking, "How hard could it be to mow the lawn?" You're already way ahead of me here. I put some gas in the lawnmower and after about twenty tries it started right up!

Maha and the kids came out to see me do it. It was the first time for them to see me do manual labor. I suppose I should be ashamed of that fact, but I've always made my living using my wits. If they could have seen me filet those fish back in Ohio they'd have a different impression of me.

I started mowing the grass in one area and then, instead of turning the lawnmower off and moving it to the other grassy area, I decided to keep it running. I figured I had a hard time starting in the first place, why should I tempt fate? I pushed the lawnmower over the rocks and pebbles area. Huge mistake! The rocks and pebbles started shooting out of the side of the lawnmower like bullets, hitting our glass sliding door, the stucco and my kids. They ran inside screaming. It sounded like someone was shooting a machine gun.

I thought for sure my neighbors were going to call Homeland Security. I can imagine the conversation: "Yes, officer, a Middle Eastern family just moved next door and the father is shooting his machine gun in the backyard." Luckily for us, the neighbors on both sides of our house were at work. That was the last time I've touched a lawn mower.

We lived in that tiny house for over three years. We loved it. John and Carole had one room, my mom had the other room, and Maha and I had the master bedroom. We had a small kitchen. I made a small office in the garage and that's where I did most of my work.

We were given a pure-bred Dachshund dog. We named him Rockie. Our family was now complete. Two kids, a dog, a grandmother, a mortgage, and an unused lawnmower. A typical American family.

We trained Rockie very well. He never bit anyone, and he ate everything. The dog would eat raw onions, jalapenos, and

Mediterranean food. Anything that fell of the dining table was Rockie's favorite food. He is a wiener dog. I had to put a sign in front of our yard that said: "Be Aware of Dog...Don't step on it!"

In 2006, we decided to move to a bigger home. We knew that John and Carole would soon not be able to share a room. We also thought a little more elbow room might be good for my mother. After closing the escrow on the house, the California housing market crashed. To this day, I haven't recovered.

A year after living in that home, Maha got pregnant again. We weren't planning on having another child, but we were open to the idea. Open or not, Tali came along. Tali is a Hebrew name that means "Oops". Not really. I joke about Tali being an Oops but actually, Tali in Hebrew means "Heaven's Dew" and what a gift from heaven Tali is. Or a wet blanket. Take your pick.

Our youngest was born with blue eyes, light brown hair (reddish) and very light skinned.

She looked Scandinavian. When she was born, I asked the Nurse, "Are you sure that's my baby? She is too Caucasian!"

I sometimes was aware of the skeptical looks people gave me when I walked with Tali at the mall. I said to myself, *I'm sure people think I kidnapped that baby. She looks nothing like me!*

What a joy to have Tali Joy. Yes, that's her middle name. She was such an easy baby. She slept at night, no crying, no problems. After taking her for her first checkup, the Doctor became concerned. Her facial expressions changed while she was listening to Tali's heartbeat.

She stopped, listened again, then looked at Maha and I, and said: "I think there is a problem with Tali's heart. I want to send you to a Specialist. You should go right away." Talk about stopping your life cold and putting everything into perspective. Somehow the housing crash didn't feel quite so important.

We made an appointment at the CHOC Hospital in Orange, CA the next day but that night there were a lot of tears and concerns. Maha was asking God why He gave us a child with a heart issue. I prayed and prayed and trusted that God would not allow us to go through a trial we could not handle. I told the Lord that I was willing to go through that valley if He was with us. I'm not any better than people who have kids with special needs and health issues. We are not exempted from that. Why should we?

The next morning, we drove to the hospital. We were quiet the entire ride from Corona to Orange. Right before we parked the car, Maha looked at me and said; "I'm OK with anything God will allow." I told her that I was OK as well. I'm not sure if either one of us really was, but sometimes saying a bold statement out loud makes it easier to believe.

We waited in the waiting room and were soon escorted by the Nurse to a room. A few minutes later, the Doctor walked in. He was an older gentleman with grey hair.

I normally start by introducing myself and telling the Doctor few jokes, but this time I was quiet. He asked us a few questions, then took our baby and put her on the examination table. He took his stethoscope and started listening to Tali's heart. He turned her around and listened some more. He then looked at us and handed me Tali and said, "Go Home. There is nothing wrong with this baby's heart."

I asked, "Are you sure?"

"As sure as I know you're standing here in front of me," he replied.

I said, "But her Doctor said she has a heart problem . . ."

"Do you want to believe her, the family Doctor, or the Cardiologist?" He said with confidence, "There is nothing wrong with this baby! GO HOME!"

"Oh, thank you Lord. Thank you, Doctor." I repeated all the way back to the car.

What a difference 24 hours makes. When Tali's Doctor said there was a problem, we never questioned her. We never thought that one option would be that Tali had no problems with her heart. All we thought of was, *how bad of a heart problem was it?*

Why do we always expect the worst?

To this day, Tali is as healthy as a horse, which is her favorite animal. She takes lessons weekly for riding English style.

Although I traveled a lot, I made sure I was home for most of the activities and birthdays. Entertainers are like Surgeons. You must be at work when they need you.

Your life has to be flexible enough to be able to do it.

When you have to be at a show, you must be there. People are waiting for you, and my wife and kids know that. So, when we plan birthday celebrations, it does not have to happen on that exact day. We can celebrate a day before or a day after depending on my tour dates.

I missed John's first play when he was in preschool. I was doing a Christmas Staff Party for Resurrection Church in Loveland, Colorado and while on stage, I felt terrible that I was missing my child's first play.

One time, when John was in Kindergarten, his class did a Daddy-Donut day. Fathers, grandfathers, or male figures were asked to come and have donuts with their kids one morning.

I was in Phoenix, Arizona getting ready to speak at a Singles

Banquet for North Phoenix Baptist Church. Maha called me and told me that John was crying because he really wanted me to be there for his Daddy-Donut day.

I couldn't make it. My flight back was scheduled for 7 AM the next morning and there was no way I could make it to his class on time. It's hearing that kind of report from your wife that breaks your heart. I was determined my son wasn't going to nail my name on a cross if I could help it!

The show went longer than planned, but as soon as I got off stage, I called and cancelled my flight, called Hertz rental car and told them that I would not be returning the rental car to the Phoenix Airport the next morning, but would drop it at Ontario Airport in Southern California. I tried to explain what Daddy-Donut day was to the clerk, but eventually gave up.

I then checked out of the hotel early, got in my car, and drove for seven hours back home. I made it home by 6:30 AM in time for John to get up to go to school. He was so happy to see me! We drove to school together and had a wonderful Daddy-Donut day. I was so tired, my eyes were shutting down, so I did something that I have never shared with anyone until the writing of this book.

While in class, they had donuts, milk, orange juice, and apple Juice. Nothing with caffeine. But Mrs. Powers, John's Kindergarten Teacher had her Starbucks coffee on her desk, I waited for her to look away, and I took several sips from her cup, without her knowledge, just to stay awake.

John felt great that morning, I felt great as a dad, but bad for stealing few sips from Mrs. Powers' coffee. Mrs. Powers, if you're reading this, I owe you a Starbucks gift card.

I was there for John's Baseball teams. I became the Assistant Coach. I was there for John's Soccer league and finally his Football. I was there for Carole's Volleyball and spent hours taking the kids back and forth to Kips Gymnastics and many other activities from Piano lessons to Horseback riding.

Once, I was dropping John at his Middle School on Main Street in Corona, CA. All he had to do was cross the street at the pedestrian crossing light and get to his school. He was in 7th grade. His backpack was over-filled with books that he needed to put in his locker. I then drove his sister to her Elementary School. Once I arrived at Carole's school, I was walking her to class when my phone rang. It was Maha screaming on the other line: "John got hit by a car. John got hit by a car!"

"When? How? I just dropped him off!" I responded.

I couldn't understand the rest of the conversation. I ran back to the car. Drove back to John's school and saw the Firetruck, the Ambulance, and the Police. All I could do was pray.

I ran to where John was lying on the pavement with Firefighters standing in circle around him. An EMT was talking with him. When the Police Officer knew I was his dad, he let me get close to John. The EMT had a neck brace around John's neck and was talking to him. I still remember it to this day.

He asked John to count from 1 to 10 backwards.

John quietly asked, "Why?"

The EMT explained and said, "I want to know if your brain is still working good."

John replied, "You should have the lady who hit me do that!" The EMT laughed and I knew that my boy was OK.

They took John in the ambulance, and I followed them to Corona Regional Hospital Emergency Room. I didn't know what happened or how it happened. All I cared about was that John was OK. I found out later that the Firefighters, the Ambulance and the Police were at the scene in less than 10 minutes. **God Bless America**.

We spent the next three hours at the ER doing X-Rays and other tests to make sure John was OK. He was. Thank God.

Later that night, I receive a call from a man who was originally from the Holy Land, that told me that he was the first one at the scene of the accident. He explained to me that John was crossing the street at the light. When it was time for him to cross, when an older lady ran the red light and hit my son. He flew up in the air and landed on his backpack.

The gentlemen told me that if it weren't for the big backpack, his head would've hit the curb and he would've been seriously injured. He jumped out of the truck and helped John sit at the curb and stayed with him until the paramedics arrived.

Praise God for his loaded backpack. He was complaining about it that morning. It became the instrument that God used to protect him.

Be careful what you complain about.

We dropped charges and we never sued that lady. It's not our thing to sue people. Her insurance paid for the ER bill. I think they gave us $4000 to buy a big gift for John.

It went to his college fund. Guilt is a wonderful thing.

During that year following the accident, John wasn't feeling great. He would wake up in the morning throwing up. We didn't think much of it. We thought it was stuff that he ate the night before that caused him to throw up.

After few months, we decided to take him to his Doctor. The first question the Doctor asked: "Was there any trauma that happened to John recently?"

I said, "Yes. He got hit by a car."

I didn't like the look on the Doctor's face. He immediately asked me to take John to Hoag Hospital and get a brain MRI. He made a call then asked us to go to the hospital. I took the Doctor aside and asked if he can give me a guess of what it could be.

He said, "It might be a brain tumor."

I prayed and asked God to spare us from that trial. "Please Lord. If you have to give him cancer, give it to me instead. Spare my son please," I prayed.

We arrived at the hospital, got to the Radiology Department and after filling out all the paper work, they took John in and put him inside a large MRI machine and scanned his brain.

The MRI Technician told us to go home and John's Doctor would call us with the results few days later. I said, "Sir, I'm not going anywhere. I want to know now. Please help us." The Technician was very kind. He asked us to wait. He sent the results to John's Doctor. I then received a phone call from his Doctor while we were at the hospital. I was so nervous. I had faith. But when it came to my children, my faith shook a little.

The Doctor told me he had good news and bad news. The good news was, John doesn't have a brain tumor. The bad news was he had a severe nasal infection that was causing him to throw up in the morning. He only needed antibiotics for few days and he should be fine.

I almost danced my way to the car. I was thankful. I praised God. I apologized for my lack of faith. Maha gave me this silly look. All along, she knew it wasn't that serious.

I don't know why God spared our child and has allowed other children to have tumors. I don't know. I don't know why he spared some kids from getting hit by a car but allowed John to be hit. I don't know. His ways are different than our ways. But I know He is GOOD. He cares about me and my family, and I trust in His decisions. I know that all things work together for good for those who love Him.

It took another year to help John cross the street. He became very fearful of cars. I remember later when I was teaching him how to drive, he would drive slowly. He would be extra careful when he approached an intersection or a light.

With kids being so fragile, most of them do make it and grow up. It is God that takes care of them and protects them. Your worrying about them will not change the path that God chooses.

John Going to College:

I received a phone call recently from a friend of mine named Chris. He is from the Bay area, CA. He didn't sound as perky as usual. He didn't give me time to guess. He proceeded to tell me that he was in tears and crying like a baby. He dropped his daughter off at college that morning and couldn't stop crying. He told me that I was the only one who could relate to him since I did the same with my son just a few months earlier.

My son, John, made it to a freshman in college. It was August 19th when we dropped him off at his dorm room at Biola University in Southern California. Although it is only 30 miles away from our home, it was a big deal for us. Regardless of how far he is from us, it was a milestone in our life. Our first baby was leaving home. After all the meals and laughs and prayers and sleepless nights, he was gone. Home was not the same.

Something was missing. A very certain someone was missing. Although he spent the majority of his days in his room on his phone his entire Senior year in High School, he was home. I knew he was home.

The room was empty now. He was gone. Even though we were still supporting him, he was on his own. The University didn't make it any easier on us. It gave us a day to spend preparing his dorm room. His mom bought enough stuff to furnish a 3-story home. There was just enough room to sleep and to walk from the bed to the door. He needed a 4-car garage to store all the stuff his mom bought him. I envy her. She showed her love and emotions by preparing his room and shopping with him. I didn't know how to show mine. I showed my love by repeating the statement:

"Here's a check for the tuition."

"Here's a credit card to use in an emergency."

"Here's spending money."

"Call me before you run out."

It was all monetary. I remembered the song, 'Money Can't Buy Me Love' by the Beatles but it can hopefully express it!

All that my son wanted to do was start his adult life. "Go ahead guys. Leave. I'm OK. I'm an adult."

The next day, the school did a Communion Night. That's when you break bread with your child, pray for them, and let them go. How terrible and mean is that? I think the school wanted to prove that parents like me who don't cry, will certainly cry that day.

Thousands of parents were praying and crying with their kids. It looked like a mass funeral. Each family crying for their loved one. Girls hugging their dads while moms were standing close by wondering where they went wrong; Boys hugging their moms while dads stood there trying to hold back the tears.

We said our goodbyes and we thought it was over, but the emotional roller-coaster just began.

We got in the car and drove away. It was quiet in the backseat. John was not fighting or bothering his sisters as he used to do. A tear came down my cheek. I don't normally cry. It's hard for me to cry. I'll bet you when I was born and the midwife (yes, I was born at home not at a hospital) hit me on my behind and I didn't cry; I laughed.

Dropping John off at college felt like returning a leased car that you had for a long time and then . . . walking home.

That is what our kids are: a leased car we got from the Dealer Himself; God. He blessed us and allowed us to lease them; to take care of them, maintain them, feed them, protect them, and wash them, but they are still His. It is His job to protect them, to guard them and do for them what we cannot do ourselves as parents.

After having the leased car for a while, we forget that it is not ours. Somehow it slips our mind that we need to return it someday. Someone else will lease them after that; their spouses.

I wish it was easier. I wish the school would've handed us a new baby and said, "Here is a new one. Raise him and bring him back in 18 years." Oh, we missed John.

And these are the words I used to comfort my friend Chris. I hope they are a comfort to you as a parent who sent his child to college, to the military, or as a parent who is about to do that.

Remember. They are a lease. They belong to the Dealer who knows more about them than you do. He knows their value and cares more about keeping them in optimum shape than you ever could.

There is an award for you — An encouragement for High School Students

I'm not athletic. I grew up in a different Country where the emphasis was on education rather than sports. The smart kids were the cool ones. Not the quarterback but the valedictorian.

It's different here in the U.S. When my son started his Freshman year at High School, he joined the football team. He and I both knew he wasn't any good at football, but, in his mind, it was the cool group to hang out with. That's where you get the attention. He hardly played. When asked about his position, he replied, "Left Bench."

His mom and I didn't want him to play. Whenever his Coach got him ready to go down to the field and play, we'd scream at the Coach from the bleachers. "Don't put him in the game!"

When it was time for the awards at the end of the season, the quarterback and the wide- receivers received all the praise. John looked at me and said, "What about me?"

As a dad, I prayed for the right words and then said, "John, every student is excellent at something. You are excellent at making movies, filming, and editing."

"But there is no award ceremony for that," he replied sadly.

"If there were one, you'd be the quarterback getting all the attention," I assured him.

A month before John's graduation, his High School decided to hold their first Annual Film Festival. Our whole family attended the award ceremony. Hundreds of people showed up. The competition was fierce, but not a single person got tackled. My kind of competition!

Several very good short films were nominated. Guess who received the highest award? Yes. John Rizkallah for best short film.

When his name was called, I looked up to Heaven and thanked God for the wise words He gave me four years earlier.

Are you a non-athletic High School student? Do you feel that no one appreciates what you do best? There is an award ceremony for you. If it has not been created, rest assured that one day there will be one for you, and you will be the quarterback. You will be applauded and appreciated.

You don't have to be good at sports to feel like a champion. Do what you love to do—what you are good at—and you will be recognized and appreciated sooner or later.

Even if all you want to do is sleep! Be the best sleeper out there. Get your Sleep Number so high that no one can break your record. Get to REM faster than anyone else. And I guarantee you, one day, someone will wake you up and give you an award.

I'm just not sure you'll be happy they woke you up!

As we hit the halfway point of my story, it should be clear to you that my prayers were answered. I have a Godly wife, wonderful children, and I'm doing what I love to do: Comedy.

God gave me the desires of my heart. Parenting is not easy, but it is rewarding. In the next chapter, you will hear about kids who didn't have good parents and parents who made bad decisions. God allowed me to go and meet them where they were.

CHAPTER 9:
LAUGHTER IN THE LETHAL INJECTION ROOM

Prisons:

One of the greatest honors for me was to be able to serve with Operation Starting Line, a ministry to inmates in prison started by Chuck Colson. Mr. Colson was an evangelical Christian leader who founded Prison Fellowship and Breakpoint. Prior to his conversion to Christianity, he served as Special Counsel to President Richard Nixon from 1969 to 1973. Mr. Colson served time in prison following the Watergate scandal. There, he turned his life over to Christ and upon leaving the prison, started his Prison Fellowship. Sometimes I wonder if I should commit a crime and spend time in prison. It could really help my ministry!

Operation Starting Line is a program of Prison Fellowship, centered around a collaborative network of National, Regional, and State Ministries across the Country that together seek to share the Good News of Christ and disciple juvenile and adult prisoners and their families.

My job was to go into a prison with a team of Entertainers, Bodybuilders, Celebrities, and Ex-offenders. We put on a show and shared the Good News of Christ with the inmates at the end of the program.

We'd all fly into a city and then were divided into several teams. Each team would have one Comedian, one Celebrity, one Athlete, and one Ex-offender. I don't know how they were able to tell me apart from the Bodybuilders, but through some miracle they managed to not confuse us. It was always good to meet the other performers and their families. We'd spend about two weeks in each city visiting every prison facility in the area.

Some of the people I met and became friends with were Mr. Universe, Marlin Darton, bodybuilder, Clark Bartram, singer. Leslie Kent, and the late, Steve Courson from the Pittsburgh Steelers.

Steve Courson bench pressed 605 pounds. Which means he could bench press my entire family. Including our dog.

You should have seen all three of us; myself, Mr. Universe, Marlon Darton, and Steve Courson working out at the gym in our free time. They were huge guys. I used to introduce Steve to people as North America. When they walked on stage at the various prisons, inmates listened. They respected them. I had to earn mine. I worked hard to get the respect of the inmates. I always did, but I had to earn it. The next time I'm booked on a tour like that I'm not going until I can bench press a car.

It was on these trips my family and comedian Tim Hawkins' family became friends. His daughter, Olivia, and my son, John, both were the same age. I also met Comedians Gilbert Esquivel, Chris Elrod, Joe Gutier and few other comics.

We laughed hard on the way to the facilities. We then went through the security section and walked into the yard where the stage was ready for us. Many workers from Operation Starting Line got there before us and got the sound and stage ready for us.

Most inmates came out to every performance. The ones that didn't were in solitary confinement or death row.

I always asked if I could go to the death row unit and share with them. I've been to so many death row units that I think I may hold the record; at least for Entertainers. I loved talking to them from behind the door. We sometimes did a special show for the inmates while they stood by their cells' doors and listened.

I remember one time recording Artist Peter Penrose sang a Capella (without instruments) where his voice echoed through the metal. It sounded like he was singing in a Cathedral. I then had to go up and make them laugh. After that we shared the hope we had in Christ.

At another time, I was speaking at a Juvenile facility in the Midwest. One 10-year-old child laughed so hard, then he cried. We seemed to connect. He had a great personality. I was not allowed to ask him why he was in prison, but he told me anyway. He told me that he shot and killed his dad. His dad used to beat him all the time and tie him up and put him in the closet. One day he got a hold of a gun and shot his dad.

Then he said the following words that I will never forget: He looked at me with tears in his eyes and asked, "Would you be my Daddy?" Those are words that can make a grown man cry. And when a Comedian feels that there are tears coming they shift into Comedy to cover up the pain. That's exactly what I did.

I told him, "I'm not a good dad. I'm very bad at sports, I work late hours, and I go on long rides. I don't like roller coasters. I don't make good money, I will be embarrassing to your friends . . . and Chuck E Cheese and I don't get along."

Somehow the prison counselor was able to explain to him that it was not an option. But it was a close one. I almost came home with another son!

The Death Row Chamber in Phoenix, AZ

One time our Operation Starting Line team was at a large prison in Phoenix, AZ. After finishing the program, the warden of the prison (that's like the CEO of the company) told me that I was the funniest man he's ever heard. He offered to take me on a tour of the death chamber. I agreed on one condition; to be treated like a prisoner going in for a life sentence. Six guards accompanied me. Two were in front of me, two behind me and one on each side. I was praying the Warden told them ahead of time that I wasn't really a prisoner!

I was shown the way to the gas chamber. It was a half-oval structure that had a door that looked like a large bank safe with the wheel. There was one chair in the middle. They took me inside, sat me on the chair, and buckled me up with the seat belt. I guess it is the law in Arizona to buckle up everywhere. They then left me there, shut the door, turned the wheel and left me there for what seemed like an hour. It was only two minutes. I'll never forget what went through my mind in these two minutes. I couldn't think about my car, my home, my accomplishments . . . etc. All I could think about is what's going to happen to me when they turned the gas on. What will the afterlife look like? I'm so glad that a few years prior to that day I secured my deal with my God. I accepted Christ as Savior and Lord, and I can honestly say I'm not worried or concerned about death. I know where I'm going based on the promises the Bible offered me.

That doesn't mean I want to die. I've had close calls in the past. One time, when my kids were young, we owned a white minivan. I was coming down from Big Bear mountain following an engagement I did for a Women's Retreat. Let me emphasize the word "Mountain!" The road was so steep; I was pushing the brakes almost the entire way down.

We had a little Barney toy that my daughter Carole loved. It is the size of a small toy poodle. When you squeezed it, it sang: "I love you, you love me . . . We're a happy family."

Well, while going down the steep hill, that dumb toy rolled down and got under me and got stuck to the back of the brake pedal. I couldn't push the brakes. Every time I pushed the brake, it started singing: "I love you, you love me . . . ."

I panicked. The car was speeding down the hill and I wasn't able to push the brakes. I thought, "Oh no. I don't want to die. Not this way! What are my kids going to explain to their friends? My dad was killed by Barney!" I was finally able to dislodge the stupid toy, so I survived, but to this day I can't watch a Barney video without breaking out into a sweat.

Back to the Gas Chamber:

After spending few moments in the chair, I was taken to the Lethal Injection bed. It was a small white room. Next to it is a small chamber that the doctor who executes the procedure stands and observes the inmate through a black glass window in order to remain anonymous.

I laid on the bed and they strapped me there, with all six guards surrounding me. Right around this time was when I thought maybe this was all a very bad idea. The Warden stood next to my head and started explaining the process to me. First, they'd insert the needle in my vein, and then inject me with 4 medications. The first one puts you to sleep, the second one stops the lungs, the third stops the brain. All three of these medications are reversible. The last one is the one that stops the heart and it is not reversible.

What I noticed is that there was a red phone in the room. I asked the Warden what it was for and he said, that the Governor can call at the last minute and pardon the criminal, and they can stop the execution. There were also a microphone hanging from the wall next to my face. I asked the Warden what it was for and he said, that I have to accept the pardon for them to stop the execution. It was not enough for the Governor to pardon me. I have to accept it.

How true is that to the pardon Christ offers us. We do have to accept it. It is up to us.

The Warden looked down at me and said, "Nazareth. This is as close to death as you'll ever get." I replied: "No, I fly Southwest Airlines all the time." The room, like never before and maybe after, erupted in laughter. The guards laughed so hard it shook the room.

I brought laughter in the most uncommon place. A lethal injection room.

I've had the opportunity to visit prisons in other parts of the World. As bad as it is in our houses of correction, **God Bless America**, our prisons are like 3-star hotels compared to some in a few third world Countries.

Mama Didn't Come

Mother Theresa once said, "The most terrible poverty is loneliness and the feeling of being unloved."

It is not good for man to be alone. There are places where I would like to be alone; in the bathroom and at the library. If you see me at any of these places, please leave me alone. Don't talk to me.

Isolation is great, but only for a short while. We are creatures that cannot live alone. Some monks commit their lives to isolation, but for the rest of us we cannot do it.

I've seen a lot of teenagers who think they are tough. They're the ones who think their mom and dad, if available, are dumb and outdated.

Let me introduce you to Jason, from Indiana's Maximum-Security Prison. Jason is a 19- year-old Hoosier. After one of our Operation Starting Line programs at the prison, members of our team walked around the yard to shake hands with the inmates. We saw a skinny, tall, blonde 19-year-old. He was in tears when we talked to him. We asked him for a prayer request and he mumbled, "Mama didn't come . . . ."

We asked him to repeat what he said, and he said, "Mama didn't come to visit me."

Then there was Natisha who was incarcerated in an Alabama prison. When we met her, she pleaded with us, "If you go to the other Women's Facility, would you find my mama and tell her I'm all right and I miss her?"

Prison is a lonely place. It makes you appreciate the people you're around.

I understand that there are people in our own families that we don't want to hang around. Sometimes you wish they were in prison with no visitation rights. But even that annoying relative would be a welcomed visitor when you've been stuck in a maximum-security prison for a while.

Take a moment today to appreciate the people that interfere with your desire to be alone. The ones you're not thrilled to see every day. Please remember, if you were in a prison for a period, you would love for them to visit you.

The highlight of my prison experience happened in Missouri at a maximum-security prison. What was different about that prison was that some of the death row inmates could go out in the yard and mix with the other inmates.

The inmates were laughing hard at my jokes. At the end of my segment, I shared the hope that I have when I committed my life to Christ. The same hope that comforted my dad when he passed away.

Once I got off stage, the inmates lined up to shake my hand. A few hugged me but the guards screamed at them. For obvious safety reasons, we were not to hug inmates.

But one inmate didn't listen. He approached me and hugged me and said, with tears in his eyes, "I'm getting executed soon. I believe in the hope you just shared with me." The guard didn't say anything. We hugged for about a minute. I shook his hand

and I knew it was the last time I'd ever see him. On this side of Heaven, anyway. He was executed few months later.

Recently, I visited Centinela State Prison in Imperial Valley, California. It is a large prison with several yards. I brought two of my Comedy friends, Gilbert Esquivel and Mark Christopher Lawrence, to join me. We had fun entertaining the inmates. One of the yards we visited was called LWPP. It stands for Life Without the Possibility of Parole. Some of the inmates in that yard arrived there at age 16 and will spend the rest of their lives in that yard. Without the possibility of ever leaving that prison.

Imagine living all your life in a prison. Your teen years, your adult life and your retirement in a prison. What kind of hope can you give to these guys? How can you encourage them? What do you do when life offers you no hope?

I prayed about how to encourage them. I heard the Lord whisper to me, in a James Earl Jones voice, "Tell them they are doing time but I'm outside of the domain of time!"

I understood what God was trying to tell me. He was asking me to let the inmates know that there is life after death. There is a punishment for their crime here on this earth but if they ask for His forgiveness they will spend the afterlife with Him.

I didn't think inmates, who mostly never finished High School, could possibly understand that, but they did, and they came to me after the show and several people assured me that they understood. One man in particular told me the following, "I've been in prison here since I was 16 years of age. I'm 48 now. Nobody has encouraged me like you did today. Thank you."

A few weeks later, I revisited the homeless shelter on 2nd street in Dallas, Texas for my annual Christmas Comedy Concert. It was my 3rd visit to that place. There were over a hundred-homeless people in attendance. Some were understandably not very happy about being homeless in December in Dallas.

I had no problem encouraging them. I told them that I was at the LWPP yard at Centinela State Prison in California with men who will never see the light of day (outside of their yard time). I asked, "How many of the homeless people here would trade places with these men?" Not a single person raised their arm. I then asked, "How many of you are happy to be homeless today?" All of them raised their arms.

I find it interesting that when we look at the suffering of others, our challenges and trials get smaller. That was the underlying message of this chapter of my life.

CHAPTER 10

I FEEL SO MEXICAN

911

It was Tuesday morning at 9 AM our time. My mom woke me up and in her heavy accent said, "Wake up. America is burning."

I ran downstairs and watched, in horror, what was happening to the Twin Towers and the Pentagon. I was glued to the television as Anchorman, Peter Jennings commented on the events of the day. I was holding my breath in fear of another attack that day. The shock was so profound.

Fear sank in. I experienced the same emotions people across America were feeling. As an American, I wept for the people who lost their lives, to see people choosing to jump to their death rather than get burned in the fire.

I started praying. Didn't know what to say other than, "God Help America."

Then the news started pointing to Middle Eastern Terrorists. Oh, no. Militant Islam had arrived on America's doorstep. We suffered from these people when we lived in Kuwait. I remember a time when I was a Freshman in High school. I attended a private all boy school in Kuwait. Christians were very few in Kuwait and when there was a religion class, we Christians were allowed to leave the class and use that period as recess.

In Kuwait, at that time, you didn't go from one class to another, you stayed in the same class with the same students, but the teachers were the ones that moved around from one class to another.

You also sat in the same desk the entire year. You didn't move around. The guy that sat behind me had a long beard, prayed five times a day, and called me an Infidel. Back when it was not hip to be an Infidel.

One time during Arabic class, the teacher was bragging about how women are honored in Islam more than other religions. I said, "No, Jesus was the first who gave women rights." That militant behind me said, "What do you know, you Infidel." I turned around and said, "Shut up. I'm tired of your hate."

A few minutes later, the Assistant Principal came to class and started cussing me out in front of the whole class. I was then asked to go to his office. When we got to his office, he closed the door, looked at me and apologized for his behavior. He said, "You don't want to mess with these people. We as Muslims, hate them." I said, "Then why did you scream at me and not him?" He quietly replied, "I don't want to deal with this . . . ."

The other time I had problems with them was when I was ready to go to the American Embassy in Kuwait to apply for a student Visa. The Militant Muslims had bombed the Embassy the day before I had my appointment. I thought it was the end of the world. Luckily, my brother lived in Scotland at the time, and I was able to fly there and apply at the U.S. Consulate in Edinburgh.

Still glued to the television, I was afraid. I prayed and prayed. I said, "God, I'm Middle Eastern. I'm a Comedian. I make money joking about my background. My career is over. What am I going to do? Will there be a backlash against me or people that look Middle Eastern?"

I knew that Faith and Fear don't go hand and hand, so I chose to have Faith that God would change the situation. God gave me a peace that morning that I would be able continue to do what I loved to do and, since people were afraid, be able to share even more about Him!

I thank God that He answered me right away. The verse in the Bible that came to me was, "For God Has not given us a spirit of fear and timidity, but of power, love, and self- discipline" (2 Tim 1:7 NLT).

I knew two things: I knew I loved Jesus with all my heart and I loved this country.

What could I do with that? I prayed and came up with the idea that would take all my fears away. I decided to start a concert and tour the Country with it. The title of the concert was, ***Proud 2 B American*** *comedy tour.*

I started re-arranging my Comedy to show people what a great Country we live in and that Jesus loves them and desires for them to know Him.

A few days before that fateful day of September 11, I received a call from a church in Dallas. I was scheduled to speak there the following Saturday, on September 15th. The Pastor called and apologized for wanting to cancel the show. He said, "I have no concrete reason, but I feel the Lord is telling me to cancel it."

Strangely enough, I was cool with it. That is so unlike me. I absolutely hate it when shows are cancelled. It's like your boss coming to you few days before the month is over and saying, "Oh, by the way, we're not going to pay you your full salary this month." Despite having put the Dallas show in our monthly budget, I was OK with it. I said, "That's fine. God will provide."

Now looking at in in hindsight, God knew what was about to happen. The airports were closed. No one could travel. I couldn't have gotten there even if I tried.

I had to do an event in Denver a day or two after they opened the airports. It was an awkward feeling. I went to the airport. I got to my gate, and I just sat there with my Bible open. People were quiet and very nervous. I was nervous. I knew some people were looking at me and wondering, "He looks Middle Eastern."

I didn't talk to anyone. I wore a cross necklace and patriotic shirts during my travels.

On the plane, I read my Bible the entire flight. I didn't reach out to get anything from my briefcase. I didn't even go to the bathroom. "Thank you, Osama Bin Laden," I said to myself, "I never thought I would be wearing depends this early!"

Later, the Department of Home Land Security was established and started the Random Check. Yes, I emphasize the word; "Random". The first year following 911, I flew 100 times. I was randomly checked approximately 900 times.

Surprisingly, I wasn't checked as much as other passengers. One thing I could never do anymore: Run through the airport! Even if I was late for my connecting flight, running was out of the question. Prior to 911, people would sympathize with people running through the airport to make it to their connecting flights. That was not the case after 911. From that point on, everyone looked suspicious running through the airport. Especially if you looked like me!

Also, I had to learn not to joke with the Airport Security TSA Officers. So many funny jokes come to my mind while going through the security, but I forced myself to shut my mouth. I think they should have Laugh Lounges at the airport once you pass the security line. Just like a smoking lounge where you go in and smoke. At the Laugh Lounge, you could go inside and tell jokes about mistaking your nail clipper for a weapon or patting you down and all the other funny things that come to mind while getting checked, but you can't share it with the Officers for fear of getting arrested.

Following 911, I started opening my show with this statement: "I'm from the Middle East, but since 911, I feel so Mexican."

It still gets huge laughs. But it was a reality. I tried to look Hispanic. At one point, I thought of starting to go to the airport with only my shorts and a Sombrero.

September 11 and the Iraqi War reminded me that I'm from the Middle East. I almost forgot. I know I'm an American. I'm reminded of that every time I look at my credit card bills. Sometimes I wish there was a loud speaker that can tell people, "Hey I'm an American! I believe in what this country stands for!"

How can I prove that? Wear a patriotic T-shirt? I did. It didn't help. I remember during the last Iraqi war, I wore a Support Our Troops T-shirt. Still people were asking me, "Which troops did you have in mind?"

My name is also no help at all. A few Middle Easterners I know tried to change their first and last names to avoid any discrimination. My last name is spelled R.I.Z.K.A.L.L.A.H. I pronounce it "Smith" for immigration purposes.

The name means the blessings of God. God in Arabic is Allah. I stopped using my last name. I didn't want people to duck when I said my last name.

Back to the **Proud 2 B American** tour. That was one of my most successful tours I ever did around the country. When I planned it, I wanted to appeal to all audiences. So, I hired a young, 19-year-old singer from Nashville named Brittany Waddel. She was originally from North Carolina but lived in Nashville with the family of her Manager at the time. I knew she would appeal to teens. I watched few of her videos on My Space and was impressed with her talent. You might know this young lady now as Britt Nicole, the popular Christian Recording Artist. We occasionally used the Browns Family and Recording Artist, Ashley Reynolds.

I also hired Jarrod Mcclintick, a young up-and-coming illusionist to join me on the tour. I suggested he make part of his last name disappear and shorten it to Jarrod Mac. I knew he would appeal to the kids. Following the tour, I hired Jarrod to work for me at my Comedy Crusade company and he later became a Pastor and started a church in Visalia, CA that is now growing. I'm so proud of Jarrod.

We started each concert with singing the National Anthem. For each city we went to, we invited a family of a soldier, who paid the ultimate price at war to the concert. We showed picture of their loved one and donated a portion of the product sales to them.

I thoroughly enjoyed that tour. We had radio stations sponsor us. American Family Radio and President, Tim Wildmon sponsored a few cities. We did events in Paducah, Kentucky at the Convention Center there, in Tupelo, Mississippi, Clovis, California, Northern Pennsylvania and many other places around the Country. I shared the Love of Christ at each concert in every city we went to.

A Middle-Eastern man honoring the troops using comedy. Only in America. **God Bless America.**

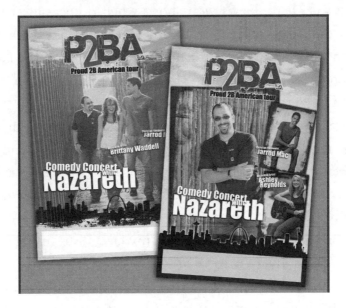

One of my proudest moments as a true American was when I was hired to perform at Nebraska Days in Lincoln Nebraska. It was a rodeo. I don't understand rodeo. Some Americans can get crazy.

Who thought of the rodeo idea? Some cowboys were sitting around doing nothing and one suggested, "Hey, let's play sports! Oh, there are no balls here to play with." And one of them misheard and thought they said, "Let's play with a Bull!"

"A bull will do," another cowboy responded. "Let's get on an angry 2000 lbs. bull. I'll get him angry and try and ride on him.

You guys try to distract it so that when I fall off his back, if I'm not dead and I still have my hat on, I win!" And that's how rodeo started.

One time I lost all my common sense and tried a mechanical bull. First it was nice. I thought, "I can do this. I'm a cowboy!"

Then it started moving faster and faster. I got seasick. I thought camels were hard. Never wear shorts when riding a mechanical bull. I did. I had a rug burn on my forehead from the hair on my left knee rubbing against my forehead. Then I was flat on the floor. My Lumbar Joint # 5 decided to leave the band "spinal cord" and go solo.

Something came out from inside my stomach, through the chest cavity, through my esophagus, out of my mouth and I bit it. Later I found out that it wasn't my tongue. It was my spleen.

I accomplished all that in 4 seconds. I felt like a bug stuck to a windshield.

At one point, before I fell flat on my face, I was sitting on the bull sideways. Like a lady. Glad I wasn't wearing a skirt.

This is the only sport when you're done, you ask the audience, "What happened?" For two weeks after that experience, I had the motor skills of a jellyfish.

At that rodeo, they parked a flatbed truck in the middle of the arena and turned the bed of the truck into a stage. The audience was sitting on metal bleachers about 100 feet away. Not a very intimate setting for Comedy.

I was introduced as America's Favorite Immigrant but that didn't get me any credibility. I started the show, and no one was listening. Almost everyone in the audience was wearing a cowboy hat. I stopped talking for few seconds to get their attention. That always works. I then proceeded with this joke. "In Nebraska if you wear a cowboy hat, you are a Cowboy. In California if you wear a cowboy hat, you're Mexican."

They burst out laughing and from that point on I had them. They laughed, they applauded, and at the end of the show, when I shared about the Hope we have in Christ, more than 10 Cowboys responded to my invitation.

America is not a racist Nation. Granted, a few individuals are. I never looked for racism and I never noticed it. I've been to rural areas around the country that have never seen an immigrant before. Yet, people were kind to me. I've been to towns that once I entered it, I changed the entire demographics of that town. Yet, people were kind tome.

God Bless America.

I'm proud to be an American and would love to be a part of movement that wants to make Americans Great Again Together! Not turn the pendulum from Republicans to Democrats every four to eight years, but to have a united America that acknowledges we do have our differences but are willing to ignore them sometimes for the good of our Nation.

CHAPTER 11

BEYOND COMEDY

Voice of Refugees

Back in 2009 I was invited by an organization that serves refugees in the Orange County Area in Southern California to perform at their annual fundraising banquet. I was excited to serve an organization that helps refugees. After all, refugees held a special place in my heart.

My mother who was born in Yafa in the Holy Land, became a refugee in 1948 at the age of 12. She had to leave her home and move down with her entire family to Gaza. They lived with relatives for a while until her dad, my grandpa, was able to get work in Gaza and buy a home.

My grandmother from my mother's side was a beautiful woman. Her name was Futna. She was named after a flower. She lived to be 94. In 1990, she came to visit her sons and daughter here in the United States from Kuwait. During her time here, Saddam Hussain invaded Kuwait. She couldn't go back to Kuwait and ended up moving to Seattle, WA with her son and two daughters.

She told me stories about my great, great grandpa. His nickname was the "Crossed-eye Lion". He lived during the Ottoman Empire. That's when the Turkish Ottomans ruled the Middle East for 400 years. During that time, in that area, Christians were treated harshly. When a Muslim walked down a street and sees a Christian coming his way, he shouts, "Go to the left, you Infidel."

Christians had to pay taxes (Jizya) to live under the Ottomans. My great-great grandfather found favor with the Ottomans and if any Christian was imprisoned unfairly, he was able to secure their freedom by visiting the ruling Sultan in Turkey.

I can't imagine the fear and the inconvenience that my mother lived through during that time of 1948 war, the displacement and the mental abuse they went through. I truly believe it affected not only her, but her entire generation.

As I've said before, my mother was full of fear. She was basically afraid of everything and constantly warned us not to rock the boat. We were told to not to do anything outside the ordinary. When we lived in Kuwait, she was fearful and kept asking us to be careful. "Careful about what mom?" I would ask. "I don't know. Just be careful." Her reply would be.

So, it was a huge undertaking for her in 1966 when she left the Gaza strip with her three children to move to Kuwait to unite with dad who had moved there a year earlier in search of work.

We didn't have any passports. All we had was an Egyptian refugee document. We had no citizenship. Most Palestinians had either a Jordanian Passport, or an Israeli Passport. We didn't have any citizenship to any nation.

That is why on May of 1991 when I became an American citizen, I meant every word I said. This is the oath I gladly made:

"I hereby declare, on oath, that I absolutely and entirely renounce and abjure all allegiance and fidelity to any foreign prince, potentate, state, or sovereignty, of whom or which I have heretofore been a subject or citizen; that I will support and defend the Constitution and laws of the United States of America against all enemies, foreign and domestic; that I will bear true faith and allegiance to the same; that I will bear arms on behalf of the United States when required by the law; that I will perform noncombatant service in the Armed Forces of the United States when required by the law; that I will perform work of national importance under civilian direction when required by the law; and that I take this obligation freely, without any mental reservation or purpose of evasion; so help me God."

I meant it with all my heart. I have a special love for this County. I love, LOVE, the United States of America. The place where dreams come true. The American Dream. Yes, I have truly enjoyed living the American Dream. In my first year in the United States I had loads of enthusiasm and determination, but not a dime to my name. I worked hard. I'll never forget what it was like to work three jobs, for three years, with no time or day off. I took no sick days or vacation days. After that, I continued to work hard and now I'm doing what I love to do. I make good money doing what I love to do: Making people laugh.

Don't you wish you could be my children and hear that story every time you complained about something? I learned a long time ago how to make my children fall asleep; I never read them bedtime stories, I'd just start with the line, "I came to the United States with nothing!" and within seconds they were out cold.

There is also another side to the American Dream. When I came to this country, I was spiritually broke and bankrupt. I didn't know anything about God. I was empty, I was immoral, I just wanted to have fun and experiment anything new without any principled consideration.

If that wasn't bad enough, I was also incredibly selfish, caring about self only. But in August of 1992, God changed all that. I went from nothing to hope in 24 hours.

My spiritual life was changed. I was adopted as a child of God. My eyes were opened to see my value in Christ. I learned that God loves me. He has a plan for my life. He is not mad at me. My sins are forgiven. Now that is the ultimate; spiritually, I went from rags to riches.

I know I say this a lot, but I can never say it enough; I love this country. I show my love for this country every time I help an American Homeless, every time I visit an American Prisoner, every time I encourage an American Soldier or inspire an American Youth.

One of things I loved doing prior to getting married was going to a Salvation Army location on Thanksgiving and help serve food to needy people. I remember one time we had over 30 turkeys donated to that location with all the trimmings and we only had few people who came to get a free Thanksgiving meal. Volunteers were standing by feeling sad that most of the food was going to go to waste. I had an idea. I asked if any of the volunteers had a car. All of them raised their hands. I suggested that we divide the food into 10 cars, drive around the city and look for homeless people who didn't have a Thanksgiving meal that day and give them food where they were staying.

We also went house to house in poor neighborhoods and knocked on people's doors and asked if they had a Thanksgiving dinner. Most didn't, but had too much pride to stop by the Salvation Army location to eat a meal. In a few hours, we passed out all 30 turkeys and all the food we had.

I tell you all this not to brag but to show you my heart. I feel so blessed to be here that I can't help but want to bless others. It's as if God has filled my heart and I get to give away whatever spills over!

So, back to my story. I was excited to do a show for an organization that was helping refugees. I went to visit the facility to see the work. I was very impressed by what they did.

The night of the Banquet, I arrived at the Hilton in Anaheim. When I got into the hallway outside of the Grand Ballroom, there were several vendors. Almost all the materials had Islamic writings on them. The Master of Ceremonies was an Imam of a local mosque (similar to a priest of a church), the Guest of Honor was the first scarfed Judge from Michigan, and they were honoring the Islamic Center of Cerritos. The whole event felt very Islamic.

I felt out of place for a while, but I came to understand this organization was not a religious organization, but they were very closely associated with C.A.I.R (Council of American Islamic Relations).

I did my show and received a standing ovation. I did an encore and that went great as well. When I left and while I was driving home, I felt a still small voice say, "You need to do this in My Name!" I slowed down the car and said, "What do you mean?"

I knew it was the Holy Spirit of God speaking to me. I just wanted clarification. I said, "You mean do a Refugee Ministry that will share the love of Jesus?"

That was it. I went home and slept like a baby.

The next morning, I went to church at Calvary Chapel Costa Mesa. In our Bible Study, Susan, an Iraqi believer in our church approached me and said: "Nazareth, we need to do something for the Arabic speaking refugees that come to Southern California. We need to do it in His Name! We should call it: Voice of Refugees."

I was shocked. All I could say is: "Oh, Lord. God was telling me about this last night."

At that moment, one of my best friends and a smart business man, Zack joined the conversation and said, "I'm in. Let's do it."

That was the start of my next adventure. Can you believe how quickly it all came together? That's right—in 24 hours!

A few days later, we met at an attorney's office and formalized our decision to start a Christian charity called Voice of Refugees (VOR).

I was assigned to be the Chairman of the Board, Susan, the Treasurer, and Zack, was the Secretary. Dorothy, a beautiful lady who's a graduate of Talbot Seminary and has a heart for Middle Eastern people, joined us as a Board Member.

Our Mission Statement is as follows, "To show the Love of Jesus Christ to needy refugees. We wanted to help refugees assimilate and become valuable contributing members of the American society."

I thought my job was just to raise money and bring awareness to the ministry, but the first few years proved me wrong. The demands for the new ministry were huge. We started using Susan's garage, we hired an Iraqi lady named Samira, a Christian from a Muslim background, to be our first employee. She visited refugees and helped meet their basic needs. On weekends Zack, Susan and myself, along with our children and spouses, helped deliver furniture to new refugee families arriving to Southern California. All three of us contributed equally to help raise money to pay Samira and cover the bills.

We then graduated from Susan's garage and rented a U-store it space. We collected donated furniture and then delivered it to refugees. We had people with trucks help us deliver it.

We received our IRS Exemption approval within months. Which, if you understand how any government works, was true a miracle. Some of my friends gave me money to help with the new ministry. Soon we were able to get our first location; a small warehouse in the city of Anaheim. It had two offices and a storage area. As soon as we moved into our new space we decided to start teaching English as a Second Language classes to refugees.

To accomplish that I needed to get permits from the City of Anaheim. I spent many days and many hours driving from Corona where I lived to Anaheim to fill out endless stacks of forms to get the permits we needed. I also had to fill out many other documents with the State and the IRS. Although I knew beyond a shadow of a doubt we were doing all of this for God and his children, I do feel a little guilty about all the trees we killed to get it going.

My calendar as a Comedian became less busy since I was too busy with VOR. In the first four years of VOR's existence, VOR was growing but my career as a Comedian was declining.

In our second year of existence, we were able to hire few employees including Joe who became our Executive Director. Which meant that then I didn't have to be as involved as I was with VOR. Susan was doing a great job keeping the spiritual aspect of VOR at optimum level. Every person that joined VOR was sent from God in the right time.

Samira left us after the first year. God sent us a great missionary, originally from Northern Iraq, named Elizabeth to help us with teaching ESL and visiting refugees. Elizabeth was a blessing to us. She since moved to Northern Iraq and started a ministry to reach Iraqi children. Knowing exactly what we needed, God then sent us Amir. Amir is an Egyptian Christian who had a heart to reach out to Muslims with the love of Jesus.

I remember one time I was in my kitchen. My mom was watching an Arab Christian Satellite TV station. They were having an interview with an Iraqi man named Fadi. While in the kitchen, I was listening in on the conversation. I didn't know why, but at that moment, the phone rang. It was Susan on the other line. Susan in her usual excitement said: "Hey Nazareth. We need to hire a guy named Fadi. He would be great for VOR. I said, "I'm watching him on TV now. Let's talk tomorrow."

We hired Fadi the next day. He is loved by all the refugees he encounters. He is VOR's first contact with refugees arriving to California. He meets them at LAX (Los Angeles International Airport). He then takes them to their assigned residence and from there, brings them to VOR to register them and then help them with their forms, going to doctor's visits, and signing them up for ESL classes.

Reem is a Syrian refugee who arrived in Southern California few years ago with her husband and two children. She didn't speak English and didn't know anyone. While walking her kids to school, she met a scarfed Muslim woman who advised her to go to VOR and take free ESL classes. Reem found her way to VOR and started learning English.

She soon connected with some volunteer Pastors that serve with VOR and they were able to share the love of Jesus with her. Although she came from a traditional Christian background, she didn't have a relationship with Jesus. She soon committed her life to Christ and started attending college. I'm happy to report she just got her degree in early education. Reem was hired at VOR few years ago to run the daycare. Reem is on fire for the Lord and does the worship time at the devotions we do.

We love what we do at VOR. We see transformations happening before our eyes.

VOR provides free furniture, classes for English as a Second Language, Job training, Computer training, Child care . . . etc. ALL FREE with no government help. Government grants come with restrictions on the freedom of sharing our faith with the refugees.

Our organization is completely funded by Christian Individuals and churches that believe in sharing Jesus while meeting the need.

We are a Christian charity. We don't choose which refugees come to this Country. We don't do any vetting. That's for our government to do. We only help those who arrive here legally.

We get calls from World Relief or other agencies advising us of the time of arrival for these families and we then go and pick them up.

We do offer a daily devotion for our refugees. It is not mandatory to attend. We do have refugees from Iraq, Egypt, Syria, Iran and Afghanistan. One of the highlights of our ministry is the Thanksgiving and the Christmas banquets. It gives them a sense of community. Most refugees lose that when they leave their home countries.

At one banquet, I was seated at a table with a Sunni Iraqi man, a Shiite Iraqi man, an Iranian, and a Coptic Christian Egyptian man. I was laughing with Pastor Pat, the Senior Pastor of Crescent Baptist Church that we rent our current facility from. I told him that here at VOR and at this table we are able to unite people that the White House and the United Nations couldn't do.

To this day, none of us, Zack, Susan, or I have benefited by so much as a penny for serving in this ministry. I hope you can see that what we have received is so much greater than any temporary monetary gain. God has expanded the ministry to where we now have six full time employees, three part-time employees, and fifteen daily volunteers!

We've served over 1,500 families in 8 years! Muslims, Christians, Sunnis, Shiite, atheists, Yazidis, etc.- all were helped. We show the love of Jesus to them while helping them assimilate into their new American home and cultural changes.

I have been asked if I am concerned about possibly aiding terrorists hiding among those we help. I personally trust in the American vetting system. 99.9% of the refugees we serve are women and children, widows and single moms. These women attend a daily voluntary devotion. What about the children?

If we can teach even one 5-year old boy about the love of Christ and about our great American values, I think, even if his father is a terrorist, we've stopped another generation from becoming radicalized.

None of the VOR staff fearfully worry about that. Neither do any of us get involved with political arguments. Jesus never worried about the Romans. If the current travel ban temporarily stops refugees from coming to Southern California, we already have so many to help and show love to. God brought them to us. We need to show them the love of Jesus—period.

Here's a letter that came from our executive director at Voice of Refugees following the news about the Travel Ban:

A RESPONSE TO THE IMMIGRATION EXECUTIVE ORDER

There has been much confusion and much misinformation circulated about President Trump's recent Executive Order titled, "Protecting the Nation From Terrorists" released on Friday, January 27, 2017.

Voice of Refugees would like to reassure those who might be concerned about the impact of this Executive Order, both on VOR and those we serve, that we are continuing to meet the needs of hundreds of recently arrived refugee families. Our food distribution every Monday, our ESL classes each Monday-Wednesday, our furniture deliveries, transportation services, driver's training, translation services, assistance with social service forms, and other services will not be interrupted by the Executive Order.

In addition, we continue to register new families as part of our over-all assistance and we will continue to greet new refugees when they arrive at the airport, including some who were in transit and cleared this past week.

To those who labor with us to serve in the name of Jesus, please accept our continued thanks and profound gratitude. It is a privilege to serve the kingdom of God alongside you. We continue to utilize a large volunteer force to accomplish the work we've been called to in His name and for His glory.

Those refugees who have been vetted through the current (normally two-year) vetting process and are one of the seven countries included in the resettlement pause, may incur a delay of up to 120 days but they are not necessarily disqualified from entry just because of their country of origin.

Syrian refugees comprised 24% of the new families we served through VOR in 2016. The ban on Syrian refugees creates an uncertainty for timing until the Trump administration can decide on the safest vetting process. We pray this process is short and will bring relief for the many displaced families originally from Syria who are living in Jordanian and other foreign refugee camps.

VOR supports the efforts to protect everyone who lives on American soil. We pray that these decisions will be reached rapidly and thus not delay the safe migration of those who have had to leave their homes and families to seek safety.

Thank you for your prayers and petitions on behalf of our ministry and His work.

Fadi's Story — Life and Death in 24 Hours

One of the godliest people I've had the pleasure of hiring is Fadi. He is a great Christian guy from Baghdad, Iraq. He's the same guy I overheard on TV that day when I was in the kitchen.

Fadi spent most of his life teaching the Word and serving at churches in Iraq. On Saturday, April 07, 2007 Fadi was returning from serving at a church in Kirkuk in Northern Iraq with two other Christians in the car when they were stopped by armed men. The men let the other two men go and arrested Fadi. They also confiscated his CDs that were with him.

They also arrested 6 other men from different cars. They covered their faces and drove them to the middle of the desert. These armed men claimed to be from the New Islamic State of Iraq and Syria (ISIS).

They ordered Fadi and the men to enter through a small hole dug in the ground, that led to a bigger hole the size of a dining table. About 4 feet in height and 6 feet in length.

Right when they got to the area, they found out that Fadi was the only Christian among the hostages.

The Prince (Amir) of the group who acted like the Judge who ordered the executions gave Fadi the option of denouncing Christ and becoming a Muslim or to be cut in pieces. Fadi looked at him calmly and said: "I will die a Christian. I will never denounce Christ." The Prince then screamed to his men, "Slaughter the Infidel."

Although his soldiers were very close to him, miraculously, God shut their ears. They never heard him. At night, Fadi and the other hostages would be pushed into a smaller hole, deeper in the ground, and the soldiers would sleep in that 4 x 6 ft. cavity.

Each day, ISIS would pull a guy out and slaughter him. On the fourth day, another prince came and asked for the American Infidel. There were no Americans there. Fadi said to him, "I'm the only Christian here." The Amir asked him again if he wanted to convert to Islam. Fadi rejected his offer. Amir ordered his execution, but again no one responded.

During that time, Fadi missed his family so much, but God was so gracious to him that he would have vivid dreams of himself being with them and talking to them.

One of the soldiers came to Fadi one day, and said, "I listened to the CDs you had. That was you teaching. I like the way you teach about the love of God." Fadi told the guy that he was praying for him and the other ISIS soldiers. He was praying that God would change their hearts.

On the 6th day, there were only two men left. Fadi and a guy named Alaa.

That morning, Fadi had the idea of escaping. Just running as far as he could in the desert. Although they were warned that there were many ISIS snipers that would kill any hostage that would run, Fadi thought he could do it.

One minute later, Alaa came to Fadi and whispered to him that they should escape. Fadi told him, "Let me talk to God and ask Him if we should do that." Alaa, was confused. As a Muslim, he didn't know what it means to talk to God.

Fadi explained that he had a relationship with God and that he felt Jesus' presence with him. Alaa desperately agreed. Fadi prayed and then came back to Alaa and said: "God told me that if we escape, we will survive, but if we want to wait for Him to rescue us, He will get the Glory."

Alaa agreed, which made Fadi very nervous and responsible for Alaa's life since Alaa agreed to God's plan and stayed with Fadi.

At that time, ISIS had contacted Fadi's family and asked for money. The family decided to send Fadi's younger brother to meet them. Everyone in their town encouraged Fadi's brother not to go. They said that it was a trap. They were sure that Fadi was dead by now and they would kill the brother as well. But Fadi's brother was courageous and decided to go.

Other Islamic terrorist groups who heard about the story called Fadi's family and demanded money and claimed that they had Fadi and that they would kill him if they didn't comply.

Fadi's brother decided to take a taxi and head towards the location where the ISIS people asked him to meet. The taxi driver drove to a point outside of town and refused to go any further. He had stopped miles from the location. He said that the road they were on was called the Road of Death and no one can survive driving on that road.

On Friday morning, The ISIS solder that was impressed with Fadi's teaching brought Fadi and Alaa out of the hole. There was a mass grave near the hole with fresh blood on the sand. Fadi looked at Alaa and said: "God will rescue us today. We will survive."

The solder then came to Fadi and asked him if he is still praying for him? Fadi told him; "Even if you didn't have a gun and we were in a different setting, I would still pray for you." The soldier then put Fadi and Alaa in the trunk of a car and they drove away. Later they stopped on the Road of Death and they let Fadi and Alaa out.

They told Fadi to look behind him to see his brother. Fadi thought for sure that they killed his younger brother, but his brother was standing there.

The ISIS soldiers got back in the car and drove away. They left the three guys in the middle of the desert to die.

Occasionally a car or two will drive by on that street at high speeds to avoid ISIS snipers. No one would risk stopping for hitch hikers. But on that day, a truck pulled over and stopped.

A man dressed in white got out of the truck and approached the tired thirsty men. He asked why they were still alive. Why would ISIS let them go?

Fadi's brother was about to talk, when Fadi jumped in and told the guy. "If you ask us, we will tell you the truth. We will not lie, but I cannot share the truth with you, so please don't ask us anything." Fadi continued, "Can you still drive us to town without asking us anything?" The driver agreed and didn't say anything. He just insisted that Fadi would call him once he got home and tell him that he arrived home safe. The driver promised to hang up the phone after that and not ask any questions.

Fadi knew all along that this man was an angel of God sent to rescue him. When he got home, he called the guy and told him that he arrived. The guy said, "Welcome home" and hung up. I guess angels have phones.

A day later, Fadi received a call from the ISIS soldier that had his number. He asked if Fadi was still praying for him. Fadi said yes, I am. Then Fadi hung up the phone and threw it away.

Fadi later moved to Egypt and from there to Southern California where God assigned for him to start working for Voice of Refugees and to show love to Muslims.

That is hope in 24 hours. On Thursday, Fadi thought he will be killed. On Friday he was free.

It is great to know that God controls the number of days we live. If it is not our time to leave this earth, nothing can happen to us. We need to have that assurance.

God still does miracles to this day. He still rescues people. Some of those survivors who escaped the persecution and the execution of militant Islamists are here in the US and they need to hear about the love of Christ and to receive help.

That's why God prompted three Middle Eastern Christians to start VOR.

CHAPTER 12
BANKING ON GOD

Hope in 24 Hours: Out of Debt

If anyone knows about financial struggle, Maha and I do. We lived with it for many years. As newlyweds and as parents we never had a budget. We didn't know how to budget. The irony is that we both have Accounting backgrounds. Maha graduated from Bethlehem University in the Holy Land with an Accounting Degree. I used to do Tax Accounting for a major restaurant company. I know Quicken and she knows QuickBooks.

The honest truth is, for some reason Maha and I cannot live on a budget. We don't know how to tighten things. Our budget is like the long balloons you make balloon animals with. You squeeze on one side; it bulges on the other side. We save on the doctor's visits and then spend the money on the dentist. You save on electricity and you end up spending more on water.

But seriously, how can we budget when our income is unstable? Some months I have a lot of shows, other months I don't. Sometimes we go for few months with very little income, so we pray harder and conserve, then we get a good month full of shows and we will indulge to make up for the hard months we endured.

Sometimes Pastors of churches cancel a show just because during their staff meeting suggested they need to get a singer instead, or the Pastor falls out of grace, commits adultery and there goes our honorarium that we were counting on to make ends meet that month.

Although we were never lavish spenders, we are much better with our finances today.

There were a lot of variables but there one thing that was solid. Early on, Maha and I agreed that we would not allow financial hardship to come between us and affect our marriage. We would not argue because of money.

This is worth repeating from an earlier chapter, for the sake of emphasizing the point. Dealing with money was easy for me, because when I was laid off my job, I came to Maha and told her the news.

I also comforted her with the fact that because of my credentials, I could get an Accounting job the next day. As you recall, she encouraged me to pursue my comedy since she would rather have a happy broke husband, than a well-off miserable Accountant.

During the Great Recession of 2007-2008, I spent many hours negotiating with Bank of America to consider lowering my mortgage. I was paying 90% of the mortgage, then 80% since I wasn't getting any work. Most churches had to lay off some of their

Pastors and it was so difficult to let them and their families go. So, the last thing on their minds was to have a Comedy Concert.

People were struggling to make ends meet so they didn't have any money to buy tickets to attend a concert.

I called the bank almost every week to see if they could give me a break. I had well- meaning Christian friends advise me to stop paying the mortgage; they told me to stay as long as I could and then when evicted, I could take the money I saved and either rent or buy another house.

Others asked me to short sale the home. Despite all of this well-meaning, but flawed advice, I knew I signed a contract with the bank. It didn't matter if the bank was totally corrupt, I had to keep my end of the deal. That's why I was praying that they would lower my mortgage by half so that I could afford it. But they did not.

The debt kept adding up. They'd tack on fees that I've never heard of, and late charges on the mortgage, and then more late fees. Then late fees on the late fees. At one point, it added up to $70,000 in one year.

I have to admit, I lost some sleep over it. Maha did not. She knew God was going to come through as He always did. As for me, I wasn't happy with God's timing. Since Jesus was from the Middle East, to me He was always late. But then again, I have a finite mind. What do I know?

I would get up in the middle of the night and have all these fearful thoughts of my wonderful family ending up on the street. On losing everything. I felt embarrassed that I couldn't provide for them like I needed to.

One day, I had a friend that I'd known for over eight years call me to chat. We talked and talked about life and ministry. Then my friend asked me, "How are you doing Nazareth?"

I lied and said, "I'm doing fine." "Are you sure?" my friend asked. I said, "Yes, why?"

My friend replied, "Because God told me otherwise. Anyway, I'm not going to ask you any more questions. Expect a FedEx tomorrow from me. God asked me to write you a check."

A check? That's nice. I hope it is over $500 I thought to myself.

Well, the next morning, still losing some sleep over the mortgage, I heard the knock at the door and the FedEx guy handed me a package. I opened the package. Inside there was a check, from my friend, for $100,000.00.

I was shocked. I just dropped on my office chair. All I could say is, "Thank you God. Thank you, Lord. Forgive me. I didn't trust you could come through for me."

I called my friend and before I could say thank you, my friend replied. "God told me you needed that much. But you didn't want to ask."

Well, I called a Christian friend in the real estate market and he recommended keeping the money and leaving the home since its value was at least two hundred thousand under what I owed the bank.

That made sense, but God told me that I should pay what I owed. So, I rejected the world's financial advice and I went to the bank; deposited the check in my account and paid the bank every penny I owed. I also paid off my car and the credit cards.

I went from lack of sleep to Debt Free (except for the mortgage). God is Good. Hope in 24 hours.

It was not on my things-to-do-today list. It was not written in my journal. It was not on my goals for that year. God came through miraculously.

I still live in the same home today. Not because of my friend. I had known that friend for over 8 years. It was because of God. He can find ways to solve your problems in ways you cannot imagine.

I need to be very clear here; I'm not suggesting that you wait until you're so far under water that the only way to make it is for God to send a miracle your way. If I even hinted at that solution, Dave Ramsey's goons would come over and break my thumbs.

I've worked hard at righting my financial hardship to insure I'll never be in the same position again. God, in his infinite wisdom, chose to sell a few cattle from one of his hills and bail me out of debt. Who knows what tools He'll use to get you on the right path. My point in all this is that God is in control and we need to trust Him in every situation. Even when it looks hopeless.

Are you worried about finances? Do you lose sleep over it? Trust in the Lord.

Because, believe me, just when we think that money is the biggest issue in life, we realize it is not. Our life is.

Read the next chapter to find out.

CHAPTER 13
THE FRAGILE LIFE

Ten minutes away from getting Killed:

By the summer of 2010, it had been ten years since my wife, Maha, had last seen her mother. Maha was attached to her mom and talked to her almost every day. When there was conflict between Hamas and Israel, and the IDF was bombing Gaza, she would speak to her mom a few times a day, and you could hear the explosions over the phone line.

Finally, we decided to go to Gaza to see her mom. To accomplish our goal, we had to overcome two very large problems. First, although Maha was an American citizen, she couldn't enter Israel through Ben Gurion Airport since she had a Palestinian ID. Therefore, she had to enter Gaza through The Rafah Border (Egyptian Border to Gaza).

The second problem was that my kids and I are American citizens, and we didn't have Palestinian IDs. Which meant we could enter through Ben Gurion Airport, but we couldn't enter through the Rafah Border.

Since I didn't want to leave Maha to travel alone, we all decided to travel to Cairo, Egypt and then do the six-hour road trip to the Rafah Border to enter Gaza.

We flew to Cairo, arrived at the busy airport and spent a day at the Marriot in the New Cairo (Heliopolis) area. The next morning, I had to go to the American Embassy in Egypt and meet the Counselor. When I entered his office, he asked me why I wanted to visit Gaza knowing that there was a great danger for American citizens to be there.

I told him that I couldn't see my wife crying every day, wanting to see her mother, and that she wanted her mom to see the grandkids she had never really met. The last time Maha saw her mom, John was two years of age and Maha was pregnant with Carole.

The counselor was sympathetic to my story, but he warned me that when I entered Gaza, I would no longer be under the protection of the United States. He further warned me that if I got kidnapped or there was any danger on my life, they didn't have the personal or the Intel to save me.

I understood that and agreed to release my rights as an American citizen the minute I entered Gaza. I raised my right arm and repeated few words after him. As I was leaving, he looked at me and said, "Good Luck. I doubt if they will let you in Gaza."

Since I was still an American citizen in Egypt, we had to get a police escort going through the Sinai desert. At that time, every

American citizen had to be protected going through the Sinai desert. So, I went back to the hotel, got the family ready and checked out of the hotel.

Soon our large air-conditioned van arrived. We started our six-hour journey to the Rafah Border with two police jeeps and 10 Egyptian police officers with AK 47s on their shoulders. There was one jeep in front of the van and another one behind it. Remember the scene at the start of "Iron Man?" That was me and my family—but without the mixed drinks.

God Bless America for protecting their citizens all over the world (except in Gaza and few other places).

I must be honest. We felt like dignitaries. John thought it was very cool. Maha wasn't thrilled. She thought it would bring too much unneeded attention to our van.

Our two drivers had long black beards and honestly, they looked like ISIS guys.

As we were crossing the desert, I looked outside the window and saw some Bedouins and started looking at the clouds. I jokingly told the kids, "Look guys, it took Moses 40 years to cross a six- hour trip. He is probably telling God, "That's not Fair! Why does Nazareth get an air-conditioned van and make it in six hours?""

We finally arrived at the Rafah border. The two police jeeps turned around and left. I knew we were on our own now.

Little kids crowded all around the van trying to sell us stuff. My kids were shocked to see that. Before that moment, I don't think they were ever exposed to real poverty. The driver advised us to let Maha in first, since it is legal for her to enter and then she could attempt to let us in. On his advice, we stayed in the car.

One of the drivers went in the border office and came out and said, "There is no way they will let you and the kids in.

Let your wife in and go and spend few days at a hotel in the city of Arish nearby."

I said, "No. We will enter."

He said, "They will not let you in."

I said, "Then let me try."

I got out of the van, walked to the officer at the gate and showed him my American Passport. He asked if I had a Palestinian ID. I declined. "No officer. I don't, but my wife does. I'm originally from this land, and I have the right to enter." He said, "No, you are not in America now. You don't have any rights here."

God Bless America

I went back to the van. The two drivers offered to drive me and the kids back to Arish after I make sure my wife made it safely into Gaza.

I refused. I said, "We will pray to Jesus and He will let us in."

The two drivers didn't like that.

I bowed my head with the kids and prayed. I said, "Lord, I want Your will, but our desire is to enter Gaza and have the kids see their grandma. Amen."

I then looked at the kids and said, "Let's go."

I felt led to get few hundred-dollar bills from my wallet and put them in my pocket. I went back to the same officer who asked me to leave, as I hid a $100 bill in the palm of my hand. I shook his hand and said, "I'm going inside to talk to the other border officers to let me in."

He looked at his hand and the $100 bill that is now in his hand and said, "Well, go ahead."

I took the kids, walked inside the big hall. When we entered the hall, I found a luggage handler, I shoved $100 bill in his hand and said, "Go get my luggage from that van and bring it and put it on that bus that is heading to Gaza."

I then saw another officer and did the same thing. He asked me to wait while he did his magic.

At that time, we noticed Maha was still at the counter arguing with four officers trying to get us in. She had the same thought to use $100 bills, but she didn't know who to give it to. The danger was obvious. What if one of them was honest? What we were doing could get us in a lot of trouble.

By then, the officer that was doing his magic was able to get us in and on the bus. Once we got on the bus and our luggage made it, we started our 5-minute trip to the Hamas Border.

I refreshed myself on the parent's Palestinian slang that I learned in my childhood and talked with authority to the Hamas officer. I said, "Hey, my parents are from here. You Sir, got to enjoy living here all your life but I had to suffer as a refugee in Kuwait for many years. You are lucky. Now It's my turn to see the land."

He stamped our passport with a confused look that said, "How did the Egyptians let you in?"

I said: "God is Good."

We were in at last! It was nothing less than a miracle. No Westerners were allowed in Gaza at that time. A few months later, my brother-in-law from Canada was reverted back to Egypt at the same border using his Canadian passport.

We then took the 20-minute drive to Rimal area (the Beverly

Hills of Gaza) where Maha's mom lived. The entire ride, on both sides, were half-destroyed buildings, sand, donkeys and grey everywhere. There were no colors in Gaza. You can sense the sadness, the desperation on people's faces.

When we arrived, I was busy unloading the luggage. Stupidly, I missed the opportunity to see and take a video of Maha and her mom hugging each other for the first time in 10 years.

I went in and nostalgic feelings hit me from 15 years earlier when I met Maha in that house. It was old back then, but it looked a lot older now.

Once you entered the gated home, you had to walk few hundred feet and go over large stairs to get to the balcony. There was an old empty fountain in the center of the front yard and a swing on the side. That was my children's only entertainment for the next two weeks.

Maha was very nervous about me being in Gaza. She was afraid some of the militants there would recognize me from YouTube and my website and figure out what I do. They would also recognize that I was aboard member of Christian Mission to Gaza, a ministry that spreads the Love of Jesus in Gaza by providing medicine and food to needy families.

I comforted Maha by reminding her that no one knew me in Gaza. No one wanted to harm me. She reminded me that we were in a spiritual war and the evil one would love to hurt me.

I said, "Yes, But God is stronger. He will protect me if anything happens."

Two days after we arrived, I had coffee with our missionary that was serving in Gaza. We stopped at a café near Yasser Arafat's old palace. It was around 9 PM. While sharing about the ministry and praying for the church there—the only Evangelical church in Gaza—my phone rang.

It was Maha on the other line. She sounded very disturbed and asked me to come home right away. I said, "Honey, Why?" She said: "I don't know. I just feel you have to come home now."

I did. I prayed with our missionary and took a taxi home. No sooner than I got on the steps to the veranda of her Mom's house, a huge explosion rocked the entire neighborhood. The noise shook the entire house. We saw a huge ball of fire in the far distance.

My kids started screaming. We all ran inside the house and shut the doors. My kids were terrified. They've never heard an explosion before. I wasn't sure what happened. We thought another war had erupted between Hamas and Israel and that the IDF was bombing Gaza again.

As a father, your main goal is to protect your family. What could I do? I'd never been in war. I've never carried a gun before. We prayed and waited. Thankfully, it was a lone explosion.

I'm so glad I came home when Maha asked me. The kids had a hard time sleeping that night. It took me longer than usual as well. I was alert to every little sound.

The next morning, Maha's cousin came to visit. Her husband was a Surgeon in Gaza. He asked if I wanted to go with him and see the location of the explosion from the night before.

I agreed. Maha was upset. "Why did you want to leave the house? Stay in," I told Maha, "Relax. Have faith." Telling my wife to have faith is like asking Bill Gates to have more money.

The surgeon took me to where I was at the café the night before with the missionary. He showed me the damage to the palace area where Arafat, who has been dead for a while now, used to keep his helicopter. The IDF claimed there were a tunnel entrance there.

These tunnels were used to transport weapons, food, and sometimes cars from the Saini to Gaza.

I told him that I was at that same café the night before. It happened ten minutes after I left the café.

Thank God for my wife and her warning. I could've been dead. Thank God that He warned her. God knew better that if he warned me, it would've taken me 30 more minutes to obey.

That Sunday, I drove to the church in Gaza. There were two Hamas police officers with long beards and AK 47 machine guns standing guard outside. I said hello and went into the church.

I asked Pastor Hanna (That's a man's name in Arabic) why they were standing there. He explained that it was for our protection. We laughed and started the worship. I then went up and preached a message in English to the congregation. Pastor Hanna translated for me. I shared about how can people be saved and why Christ came to Earth. For the first few minutes of my message, I shared some jokes from my act and they laughed. I was shocked that they laughed. Those Christians were under intense pressure religiously and politically. But they laughed.

It amazed me how we in America allow little things to upset us and take our peace away. But there in Gaza, in one of the poorest and most populated place on Earth and under so much pressure from Hamas and Israel, the Christians could still laugh.

One of the congregation members later told me that the presence of God in Gaza was amazing. They felt His protection and His grace continually. They didn't have much but they had Him.

Maha was fearful for me going to the church and preaching. It seemed like the roles were reversing. In the US, Maha was the one with all the peace and faith and there in Gaza, I was the one telling her to have more faith.

Maha's older sister from Baltimore, Azza, was there at the same time and her four kids were at the same house with us. Every morning I would take them to the roof of the three-story house and we would have a Bible study.

Then, every morning, Abu-Ahmed, the grocer, came by with his cart pulled by his donkey. On the cart, he had different produce; cucumbers, tomatoes, apples . . . etc.

It was like a Farmer's Market on Wheels. Maha's mom would go down and buy some produce while Tali, my youngest daughter, age 3 at the time, and Carole, age 10 would ride the donkey. For a little tip, Abu-Ahmed would take them for a ride around. The kids were having a great time. They played on the swing, filled the dirty fountain with filthy yellowish water and jumped in it.

I was disgusted. I thought to myself, I spent hundreds of dollars on annual passes to Disneyland for my kids and they were having more fun in Gaza! What was wrong with them?

One morning while sitting on the balcony, John, age 12 at the time, Carole, and their cousin Kareem, age 7, wanted to cross the busy street in front of the house to get to the grocery store and buy some candy.

I don't know why I agreed. They walked to the front of the yard, opened the gate, and few seconds later, I heard the screeching brakes of cars and people screaming.

I jumped off my chair, ran to the front door, opened the gate while praying and I saw this busy street completely stopped. I looked and saw Carole on our side of the street. She had refused to cross. John and Kareem were standing on the other side of the street.

Some people came out of their cars.

What happened I shouted to John. He said, "One car almost hit me and Kareem. We don't know how it missed us."

"Thank you, Lord." I whispered to myself. One guy told me that a car hit the boys and just kept going. He was shocked that they were OK.

Maha and her sister came running and crying. I comforted them and told them that everything was OK.

A few hours later, there was a knock on our front gate. Two men were at the door. One told me that he hit one of the boys and he was afraid to stop so he went and got his brother who is a Doctor and wanted to know what happened to the boy. I told him that everything was OK.

God saved them. I was so mad at myself for letting them cross a busy street like that. Jay-walking in any Middle Eastern busy street can be deadly.

After that incident, Maha just wanted to leave Gaza. She was too stressed. In one week she almost lost her husband and her son.

It took a few days to get to the border in Gaza to try to leave. I needed a permit to leave. The Rafah Entrance was closed and very few people were allowed out.

I went to one office near the border and attempted to wait in line. There was no such thing as standing in line.

America taught me the whole standing in line thing. When I lived overseas we didn't stand in line. It was the guy with the strongest shoulder who made it to the window first.

Living in America taught me to respect other people and that we are all equally important. So now I stand in line and wait for my turn. But I now expect everybody to stand in line. Don't cut in line in front of me. Americans are very kind and gracious people until you cut in line in front of them. Then they will hate you.

People will only cut in line for things they want. You don't see people cutting in line for signing up to donate body parts or taking a vaccine.

I remember in elementary school, back in Kuwait, we had to stand in line to receive a vaccination. That was the only time people stood in line. Imagine standing in line for an hour not to enjoy a ride or receive a benefit but to inflict pain on yourself. By then you've destroyed yourself from worrying. That gives you an hour in line to think of the upcoming pain. I'm a baby when it comes to shots. It's not a bad thing. It kept me from doing heroin.

Well, needless to say, at this border office, nobody wanted to stand in line, people were crowding the counter with their passports in their hands waving them right in the face of the window employees, attempting to get their attention.

I couldn't do that. I just stood there trying to figure a way to get my passport into the hands of a border employee.

At one point, one police officer started screaming at the people to back away from the counter and sit down. That they would call their names and serve them. Nobody paid any attention. Then something happened that shocked me; the office took a long stick and started hitting the people crowding the counter.

He finally managed to get everyone to sit down. It was sad. A few seconds later, while people were sitting, new people walked into the office and went to the counter and handed the employees their passport. The employees accepted and stated serving them. That's when the people who were forced to sit jumped up and ran to the counter. The cop just gave in after that.

God Bless America for the order that we have here. You wait in line, take a number, respect other people . . . . etc.

I went back the next day and the day after and the same thing happened. On the third day, I waited for one of the supervisors to leave the counter. When he walked outside I stopped him and shook his hand. Guess what was in my hand? Yes, you guessed it. A $100 bill. He asked for our passports, went inside and asked me to wait.

A few minutes later, he came out with the permit.

The next day we packed our bags. It was 10 days earlier than planned. Despite that, we headed to the border with Maha's sister and her kids.

I saw the same guy that helped me the day before. I gave him our passports with the permits. He went inside the large hall where I spent the last three days trying to get a permit.

I was totally unaware that John my son had followed me. I just wasn't paying attention. I was keeping an eye on the guy who took our passports.

John came in crying. I asked him what was wrong?

He told me that a police officer stopped him at the entrance of the hall and asked him if he was a Muslim.

John said in English, "No, I'm a Christian."

The officer then told him that unless he says the words: "There is no God but Allah and Mohammed is his messenger," he would not let him in the hall.

John said, "But my dad is inside." The officer insisted, and John repeated the statement and came in. I was furious. I was so angry. For the first time, in my life, I wanted to smack someone so bad. I wanted to smack this officer so hard. Turning the other cheek was not an option. I proceeded to walk to him, but something stopped me. It was the voice of reason. I didn't have our passports with me. They were with the other officer.

We were in Hamas country. We were Christians. And the US could not help me.

Oh, it was so difficult to control myself! John asked me if he had become a Muslim by repeating that statement. I said, "No, that is stupid."

I waited few more minutes and then the officer who had our passports came out, handed me the passports and asked us to get into a bus that was heading to Rafah.

We got in the bus, then waited over two hours inside the hot bus to leave to Rafah. It was a 5-minute drive.

Finally, we got to the Egyptian border, and from there, came out of the Rafah gate where a large air-conditioned van was waiting for us. We got into the van and drove away.

We prayed in the van and thanked the Lord Jesus for getting us out of Gaza safely. We spend the next 6 hours singing and laughing.

Because our flight back home to America couldn't be changed, we spent nine days in Egypt enjoying the pyramids, the food, and the people.

I nearly lost my life as well as my son's life in Gaza.

Life is precious. It is our priority. When your life or the life of your loved ones are in danger, you don't worry about bills, cars, homes or making a good impression on others, you just try to stay alive.

Keep reading to see how I got the honor to honor the men and women who risk their lives daily for our freedom.

CHAPTER 14
AMERICA THE GREAT

Ramstein Airforce Base

The Speed train was crossing Germany, from Ramstein Airforce base heading to a small town to board a river cruise on the Rhine river. Everyone was quiet on the train, sleeping, reading, staring, except for me and Mark Gungor, Pastor of the largest church in Green Bay, Wisconsin and author of the book: Laugh Your Way to a Better Marriage.

Mark's the son of a Puerto Rican mother and a Turkish dad. He's also one of the funniest and loudest people I know. You cannot be around Mark and not laugh. What I love about this man is that he is immune to criticism. It does not bother him at all. He believes in what he preaches and loves life. He is also tenacious. His lovely wife Debbie fought stage 4 cancer 5 times already. Still, they are the most joyful people to be around.

A German man walked by us, unamused by our loud conversation said to us in broken English, "You must be Americans!"

We proudly replied, "Yes we are!" He shook his head and left.

In Germany, it costs you ½ Euro to use the public restroom. You must insert it in the locked door of the public bathroom to gain access. If you don't have change, you'd better bring a change of clothes with you.

We arrived at the boat and spent the day cruising the Rhine river looking at the castles on the shores of the Rhine. Some of the castles had been partially destroyed by Napoleon Bonaparte the French Military and Political Leader. That was several hundred years ago. You'd think someone could have gotten around to fixing them by now!

That evening we arrived back at Ramstein Air Base to sleep.

The next morning, September 11, 2011, I was seated at Ramstein Air Force Base Air field, next to the General of the US Armed Forces, Admiral of the US Navy and dozens of high-ranking officers at a ceremony to commemorate the victims of 911. The night before, I performed for 1000 airmen who had just returned from Iraq.

We stood there in honor for the Flag-Folding Ceremony. It took our airmen two minutes to fold the American flag. Then they played the German Anthem and the German Airmen folded the German flag. It took them 15 minutes to do that. The General appeared frustrated with the time it was taking to fold the German flag.

That's when the comedian in me had to say something, so I leaned close to his ear and said, "Aren't you glad they don't fold your LAUNDRY?"

You should see a Four-star general trying not to laugh. He started shaking and his shoulders were going up and down. After they finished he shook my hand and gave me the "Please don't do this again" look.

Following September 11, 2001, I was very afraid about what was going to happen to my career as a Comedian. Ten years later, I was invited to speak to 1000 Airmen at Ramstein Airforce Base in Germany to commemorate the 10th Anniversary of September 11.

Personally, I find it amazing that God would arrange it to have me sit next to Generals and Admirals from the United States Armed Forces.

God Bless America.

If today you are afraid about something in your life, please lay it before the Lord. Trust in His plan and ask Him to give you His peace—the peace that surpasses ALL understanding. You don't know what tomorrow can bring.

That evening I performed for the troops, then Mark did his seminar. That night, I was heading to my hotel room inside the compound. I entered the elevator with two ladies that just returned from Iraq. They looked tough, no facial expressions, I looked at them and said: "Thank you for what you do, for your sacrifice, it means a lot to me. I'm from the Middle East. I grew up in Kuwait and I appreciate what you do." They teared up and one of them said, "It is so nice to be appreciated. It seems like nowadays, people don't appreciate what we do anymore. But thank you for saying that."

The next morning, Mark Gungor and I insisted on visiting The Wounded Warrior Hospital (Landstuhl Regional Medical Center). We wanted to say thank you to those men and women that suffered so much.

We were accompanied by two Chaplains. We visited the first room. I saw a young man, probably 19 years of age. He was lying there in bed. One of his legs was amputated.

We introduced ourselves and I asked him where he was from. He said he was from Chicago. I asked about his injury. He said that he stepped on an IED in Afghanistan. I then asked what his plans were after leaving the hospital. He said, courageously, that he wanted to go back to Afghanistan and fight with his squad.

I was moved by his reply. What a great heart to serve our Country! I was at a loss for words but then said, "Well, at least in Afghanistan you know who is shooting at you. In Chicago, you'll never know. Could be the gangs, the cops, or your ex-girlfriend." He burst out laughing, thanked us for coming and we moved to the next room.

I felt so proud to be an American. To be associated with someone like this young soldier. That kid didn't care if I was a Republican or a Democrat, Liberal or Conservative. He would give his life for all Americans. I would do the same as well.

CHAPTER 15

LAUGHTER FOR ALL

Laughter For All

wanted to call my latest tour "Free to Laugh." The name says it all. I want people who cannot afford to go see a live concert, pay to watch a Comedian live or go to the movie theatre because of financial hardships to be able to attend a large-scale comedy and music concert for free.

I also wanted to call it "Laughter For All" because I want the entire family to attend and laugh together. Families that laugh together stay together. It is rare for a family here in America to sit together and watch the same program and laugh at the same jokes.

The teens are in their rooms watching Snapchat videos or YouTube videos and laughing. The kids are on the computer playing their games. Dad or mom are watching Facebook videos or a sitcom and laughing. But never together. Never at the same jokes.

Comedy has gotten so raunchy and dirty to where a dad cannot take his 18-year-old daughter to watch live Comedy. A mom cannot invite her mother or grandmother to see the same show.

"Laughter For All" was the solution for that. Ironically, the previously copyrighted name "Free to Laugh" was too expensive to buy, so I went with "Laughter For All."

It all started 24 some years earlier while I was driving northbound on the 405 freeway in Orange County. I had a vision. Yes, me a Christian who attended a Southern Baptist Church and Calvary Chapel saw a vision. It was for few seconds only. I saw a large stadium filled with people laughing and then some of them were coming down to the field to turn their lives to God. That was it. Only a few seconds long. It had to be a short vision. I was in heavy traffic. Any longer and I would have had a vision of a fender bender.

At the time, Harvest Crusades with Greg Laurie were doing large scale crusades at the Angels Stadium in Anaheim, CA. I thought that was my answer. God wanted me to join the team of Harvest and eventually was going to have me speak there, make the people laugh, then give them an opportunity to come down to the field and have people pray with them.

So, I volunteered to become a follow-up Counselor at the Harvest Crusade. I did that for several years. One year, I invited my friend Iris. Iris was a beautiful young blonde that I worked with. She lived with her grandma. Iris was a good girl but on one crazy night, she had a one-night stand with a guy who gave her HIV, which turned to full blown Aids.

I used to pray with Iris and she attended the Crusade with me. I carried her IV bag and when the invitation came, Iris decided to go down to the field and turn her life to Christ. I went down with her. I was sharing with Iris at lunch, at the restaurant company where we both worked, about what God has done in my life and how He gave me a purpose and how I now knew without a shadow of doubt that if I died, I would go to Heaven. I was going to make it, not based on my good works, but Christ's obedient work on the Cross on my behalf.

That night I nudged one of the camera people recording the crusade to take time to interview Iris and share her story—with her consent of course.

I must admit, to this day, Harvest Crusade leadership or Greg Laurie have yet to invite me to perform at the Harvest Crusade. Evidently, he didn't see the same vision I did.

In 2013, the vision came back, and I started looking for a stadium. I didn't have the money, but I knew God will provide for His work. I wanted to rent a stadium in a poor area. I wanted the under-resourced to attend. I wanted people who didn't have Christian friends to come to the event and not feel threatened. I didn't want "Laughter for All" to be a religious event but an event that offered hope.

God lead me to San Bernardino, CA. The largest poor city in the USA according to some resources.

I drove around the city and prayed. I ended up in the parking lot of the 66'ers Baseball stadium. The Stadium can seat 6000 people and that was a good start for my leap of faith. If they had been called the 666'ers, I would have kept on driving.

I walked around the stadium and started dreaming. It was a start. In 5 years, we could build and grow until we were large enough to rent out the Rose Bowl with 80 thousand seats. God can do anything.

God Bless America. It's a free country with freedom of religion and no one can stop me.

Hey, in my book, either go big or go home!

I went back to Pastor Mike Long, my friend, sounding board, advisor, and many other titles he doesn't care to take responsibility for.

Pastor Mike was one of the Executive Pastors at Crossroads church in Corona. He became one of my board members at Laughter for all, alongside my friend and one of the best attorneys Colorado has ever produced, Michael Reagor as well as Jeff Rajcic, a very smart business man and a wonderful thinker.

Jeff attended one of the comedy classes I was teaching and we developed a friendship from there. Jeff always encourages me and insists that I'm under-selling myself. He's always after me to charge a lot more for what I do. I believe him, but I don't. If you know what I mean.

One of the best things I credit myself with is that I surround myself with smart people. People from various walks of life that I can seek for wisdom when I need it.

By faith I booked the stadium. I immediately formed the "Laughter For All" team. It was Pastor Mike Long as the Logistic manager. His son Tim Long, who was the Event Manager at the Los Angeles Fairgrounds in Pomona, CA. as our Event Manger. Robert Southward, a Godly man that I prophesized over.

I'm not a prophet, but I did have a vision while looking over The Valley of Armageddon in Israel. Robert was working for the Outdoor Channel and I told him and his wife that he would soon be a Pastor. Guess what Robert does for a living now? He is one of the Pastors at Crossroads Church in Corona, CA finishing his Theology degree. Robert was our Stage Manager.

We also have David Sanchez. David used to work for ABC Television. He left following his refusal to work on a show that was morally inconsistent with his faith. I respect David. He is a good man. He does all my videos. He oversees video productions for LFA.

Add to that wonderful team Kristin Xander Flores, a young lady from Arrowhead. Her mother took one of my Comedy classes and we became friends. When Kristin heard about our LFA event in San Bernardino, she offered to help us. And help us she did. She contacted all the churches in the area and handled the Marketing for us.

With a team like that, I looked good. I also became more relaxed knowing I had people around me that knew what they're doing.

I saw a Pastor on TBN talking about San Bernardino, CA. His name was Pastor Marco Garcia. He's currently the Senior Pastor of The Way World Outreach in San Bernardino. I knew that If I could meet him and get him involved, it would help our outreach.

He was a busy man and it was so difficult to get a hold of him. I was able to schedule a breakfast meeting with his brother and Assistant Pastor, Robert Garcia. That morning while having breakfast with Robert, Marco Garcia showed up at the restaurant and said, "God wanted me to be here." The two of them ended up being very instrumental in making the first outreach a success.

After all of this, I knew from the bottom of my heart that it was God's will to start "Laughter For All."

I immediately approached my friend and Award-winning Christian Rap Artist T-Bone. When he found out that we are trying to reach out to hurting people and offer them a free event, he jumped on board. T-Bone has performed at every Laughter For All Outreach I've done so far.

Next, I reached out to a wonderful Entertainer, Dennis Agajanian, seven times Entertainer of the Year. He performed at the Billy Graham and the Harvest Crusades. According to Armeniapedia, he is recognized as one of the best acoustic guitar players of his time. He is also an alumnus of the "Guinness Book of World Records" as the fastest flat picker. Whether playing Country, Bluegrass, Classical or Rock, audiences often find themselves in awe of his gifted ability to play the guitar.

The reason I chose these Entertainers was because they could perform in both English and Spanish. Most of the audience in the low-income areas we target are from an African-American or Spanish backgrounds.

I then invited few of my funny Comedians such as Gilbert Esquivel, Cizzle C, and Cleto Rodriguez to help me bring laughter to hurting people. Everyone got paid. I didn't want Entertainers to have to do it for free.

Gregory Hooper, the Creative Arts Pastor from Sunrise Church in Rialto, where I used to have a Comedy Club for two years, brought his band and his team and we had our first Crusade.

It was wonderful. We had 5000 people attend. I was shocked. We had two stages, one for "up-and-coming" Comedians and then a main stage. My friend, Mark Chow, who served with Foundation for Kids, provided us with 1000 toys and 1000 food bags.

We had over 150 volunteers from various churches and Calvary Chapel San Bernardino provided us with Security.

It seemed like all my California friends and family were there. Maha, John, Carole and Tali were running around helping. My church family was there serving. KSGN radio station promoted the event. Everything went as expected. The stadium was full of people, mostly non-Christians.

We told the stadium that we didn't want to serve alcohol, but they forgot to tell the concession stand staff. People were buying beer and drinking it while watching the show. Some volunteers came to me and said, "What do we do with the people drinking beer in the stands?" I said, "Leave them alone. Those are the people we are trying to reach out to." I'm was just glad they showed up.

After all the performers did their sets, I went up and did 30 minutes of Comedy and then shared my story with the audience. I told them what God had done in my life. I shared with them how God loved them and wanted to have a relationship with them. I was blown away when over 250 people responded to the invitation that night. They came down to the field where 100 follow-up Counselors and Pastors from local churches were waiting for them. They prayed with them and offered them Bibles.

While people were leaving, my team and volunteers handed them free toys and food bags. Everyone was happy. We had a great first Outreach.

In October 2013, "Laughter For All" partnered with Crossroads Church in Corona, CA to do an outreach event for the community called "The Sweet Laughter." "Laughter For All" wanted to give under-resourced people in the community an opportunity to attend a High Caliber Concert with Award Winning Comedians. Crossroads wanted free candy to give away at their Trunk n' Treat outreach they do for the city on their Halloween alternative night. They normally get over 10,000 people to attend. Crossroads always does state-of-the-art events. They are well produced. Some of the plays they produce, you'd think you are on Broadway. Their Christmas Lights event makes you believe you are in Vegas watching Cirque du Soleil. "The Sweet

Laughter" event was no exception. The quality of the show had to match the expectations and standards of Crossroads.

One father told me few days later, with tears in his eyes, that he was feeling bad because he could never afford to take his children to a concert. He couldn't afford it. So, when he heard about "The Sweet Laughter," he got excited and invited his family. They laughed together.

We have done "Sweet Laughter" every last Friday of October since. We had at least 3000 people each time.

In 2015 God was telling me to go to Vegas. Vegas has a lot of poor people. Don't be deceived. If you drive 10 minutes away from the Strip, you will be faced with poverty and deprivation. I drove to Vegas and looked for a stadium. I found the Cashman Center. It seats 10,000 people. I got excited. I met with the Event Manager. She was a sweet young lady. We decided on a date for the event.

I invited my team to meet their team in Vegas. I flew in our Stage Company Manager, Brian Jackson, and I drove with Pastor Mike to meet with them. We had a great meeting and agreed on everything. A few representatives from the city of Las Vegas were there and were impressed by our desire to do something for the city of Las Vegas for free.

They kept asking, "How much are you charging? What's in it for you?"

I kept repeating the same thing, "We want to bless the city."

We started the planning and we were waiting for the contract from the city. A month later, I received the disappointing news. The Cashman Center didn't want to do the event. I was paying them $10,000 to rent it but they told us that the Baseball Team Managers didn't want us to do the event there.

In desperation, I looked for another venue in Vegas. I wanted to do the event in May. I couldn't find another venue that was available. One day while I was having a meeting with Pastor Mike at his home, I found the Henderson Pavilion. I didn't know it existed. It was a 10-minute drive from Las Vegas in the City of Henderson, NV.

I called the Pavilion, and Dianne Mizelle, the Manager, answered the phone. I introduced myself and told her what I wanted to do. The date I was looking for was available. I wasn't sure if I wanted to do the event in Henderson since it is not a low-income area. It is more middle-class than we were looking for.

Dianne bent over backwards to accommodate us. We had one of the easiest events there. I invited Recording Artist, Crystal Lewis to perform that event. Her daughter Izzy Ray performed as well alongside T-Bone, Gilbert Esquivel, Cizzle C, and myself. My friend and Accountant, Dave Christiansen, invited his band and did the worship for us. It was a great night.

At the end of the evening, we had a great number of young people come forward to response to the message. The stage was filled with young people, old people, gang members, and more.

Over 3500 hundred people attended the event. That night Celine Dion was not performing at Caesars Palace, so we can comfortably assume that we had the largest attended show in Vegas that night. If Celine happened to attend our show, she did it in secret. At least I'm sure, she didn't come forward.

That night meant so much to me. Twenty-three years earlier, I was performing at the Aladdin Casino in a much smaller venue. God decided to keep me as a Comedian and to bless me with much better venues than the ones I used to perform in. Sometimes people are afraid that when they surrender their life to God, He will send them to Africa or make them do weird stuff. I don't think so. I think God will use whatever you are good at to honor His name, to bring Glory to Himself.

I'm so thankful for that. I can't imagine myself doing anything else than Comedy. Frankly, this is my only skill set. Well, that and filleting fish with an electric knife but I don't think I could support a family with what I earned doing that.

On the fourth "Sweet Laughter" we did in 2016, this is what happened:

Fifth Hope in 24 Hours: Blessing a family

A few days before the 2016 Sweet Laughter concert at Crossroads Church in Corona, CA, I was doing my morning quiet time with the Lord reading the Bible, God whispered to me and nudged me to bless a needy family or a single mom at that week's "Sweet Laughter."

I was a little confused since at these events towards the end of each event, I normally ask cancer survivors to stand up and remain standing. I then asked the audience if there is anyone who is going through chemo-therapy; afraid to get cancer because their parents had cancer, or afraid to do a blood test since they fear they may have cancer or just fearful about the whole thing.

I ask them to look around, to look at the people standing up and be comforted in knowing that they can survive cancer as well. That if you're going through it, there are other people going through the same thing you are. I then ask the people standing up if their life is better now after surviving cancer than before they had it. Almost all people agree that their life is much more fulfilling now than it was before.

I then asked people who had a financial crisis. People who had lost their business, job or home at one time or another, but now they are doing better financially. They're back where they were or maybe doing better. I ask them to stand up. I then ask the audience members who are afraid to lose their business, their job or their home, to look around and know that there are other people who've been through it and survived it. That even if there's a possibility that they might lose their business, job or home there's hope they can turn their life around.

Finally, I ask couples that, at one point, thought that their marriage was going down the drain; that there's no hope for them. But then decided to be selfless; to pray together; to ask God to help them in their marriage, and their marriage is thriving now. I ask them to stand and then I ask couples in the audience who are concerned and fearful about their marriage to look around and see that even if they think they've hit rock bottom and even if they think there's no hope for their marriage, to know there are other couples that have been there and done that and their marriages are thriving now.

My goal from doing all this is to take fear away from people; for the audience to have some peace of mind knowing that other people go through the same problems they go through and they get their prayers answered.

That is why I was confused. I was planning to do the same thing I always do at these large concerts, but God had a different plan. I didn't know how to share that with the church. What would they say? How would I go about it?

I didn't give it much thought the next day. The evening of the show, after all the Comedians went up and performed, I went on with my show making people laugh. Thirty minutes into my act I blanked out. I couldn't remember anything. All I could think about it Is what God told me to do.

So, by faith I proceeded to ask the audience if there was a single-mother or a family that was hurting financially. Very few people raised their arms. I looked at the people in the audience and picked a lady who raised her arm. I asked her to come up to the stage. It took her a while to come forward. I noticed that she brought her seven-year-old daughter with her. Her daughter had a prosthetic leg. She could hardly walk. The mom and daughter walked slowly up to the stage. When they approached, the steps leading to the stage, I hugged that little girl and then I looked at the mom and asked:

"Are you having a hard time financially?

She said, "Yes."

I then proceeded to ask how much is your rent?

She said, "$2000."

I then asked, "How much of it do you have?"

She said with an embarrassed look on her face: "Not much."

The Sweet Laughter event was on the 28th of October. Rent should be due in few days. So, I looked at the audience and said, "God told me to bless this family tonight!"

I continued, "We are going to cover her rent for this month. I will start with a hundred dollars from me." I continued, "If you would like to give, raise your arm and we can have a few ushers with buckets go around and collect the money."

I saw many hands go up. Some with checks, others with cash. It took about ten minutes to collect all the money from the 3000-member audience.

I thanked the mom and daughter, and I told them to go to my autograph signing table after the show and to know that every penny that was raised would go to them.

At the end of the event the mom and her daughter came to the lobby of the church and thanked me. They admitted to me that they were worried how they were going to pay the rent for this month. But that night the audience raised over $6,200 for them.

Hope in 24 hours!

I thanked them. I was so delighted to hear their story since I was afraid it wouldn't work. What if nobody raised their arm? How embarrassing would that be? But then again, I learned in my walk with God not to question Him nor doubt Him even though I don't know how to go about doing what He's asking of me.

That night one family's finances had changed in 24 hours. If you're curious, you can go to my You Tube channel and watch what happened that night. Go to *www.YouTube.com/Nazzman1*

God Bless America not only for the ability to do anything you want or imagine doing, but also for the many ways you can bless people. I learned how to give from Americans. Growing up, I knew that Americans were the most generous people. They always gave to missions, they supported third world Countries, and were the first offering relief when disasters hit.

"Laughter For All" is another American way of helping people. Putting a smile on the face of some people who have forgotten how to laugh. That may sound crazy, but in hard times we all forget the full value of laughing at a good joke, at life, or at ourselves.

CHAPTER 16

OH BROTHER!

Sixth Hope in 24 Hours

My wife Maha has a wonderful Persian friend. I'll call her Sheila. She is a former Muslim who put her faith in the Hope of Jesus Christ. She lives in Orange County, CA.

Ever since she converted to Christianity, her family abandoned her. They would not talk to her or have anything to do with her. Sheila had a great relationship with her brother. He also lived in Orange County and that relationship was shattered since her conversion. Sheila shared with Maha her sadness over losing her brother's love. Not only they were siblings, but friends as well.

Sheila cried to God to heal that relationship. For over four years, she prayed to be restored to her brother. Finally, one day, last December, she said to Maha, "I just gave this issue to God today. I'm going to leave it to God to fix this. I give up!"

The next day, she went shopping at South Coast Plaza in Orange County, CA.

South Coast Plaza is French for, "We can't afford it!" This mall separates the masses by their tax bracket. The wealthy ones go to the 3rd floor with the Louie Vuitton, Saks Fifth Avenue, and Prada. The second floor is for the middle class and includes Nordstrom, Bloomingdale, and Macys. The first floor for the lower income and that limits them to Sears.

While shopping at South Coast Plaza, Sheila was making her way through the crowded mall full of Christmas shoppers to get to Corner Bakery restaurant. Just then, she slammed into someone. She looked up and as the gentleman she hit turned around, Sheila was shocked.

You guessed it, it was her brother. Out of thousands of shoppers, she slammed into her own brother. I mean, come on! Even if you're not a believer, that's pretty amazing! But that's exactly the kind of minor miracle God loves to orchestrate every day — if you allow Him!

Her brother looked at Sheila and smiled. They hugged. He then asked her to have coffee with him. They spent the next four hours catching up. A relationship was restored in 24 Hours.

Are you praying about a restoration of a relationship you cherish? Give it to God. Let Him restore it. He is in the business of restoration.

CHAPTER 17

OVER-THE-COUNTER COMEDY

The Healing Power of Comedy

I arrived in Seattle Tacoma, Washington airport early. I had few hours before my show in Poulsbo, WA. I arranged for a meeting with a young man named Doc, who wanted to do Comedy. He tried few times but wasn't sure how to proceed. I told him I'd meet with him and maybe we could drive together to Poulsbo. I picked him up and invited him to dinner. We talked about Comedy and his desire to do it.

I love doing that. I love to help younger Comedians who desire to do clean Comedy and to honor God with their talents.

One of the things that I know I'm good at, and can communicate well, is my experience in Comedy. I started teaching

Comedy back in the 90's teaching at the LA College in Los Angeles, CA. I had Surgeons, Nurses, Attorneys, and Business people in my class.

After the end of the semester, they got to perform at graduation. I later taught several classes at different churches.

Comedy for some of my students was more like therapy. When asked to make fun of themselves as a homework assignment, many people started talking about their issues for the first time. And in trying to make it funny, often doing jokes about their situation opened their eyes to the real issue. I've seen many students graduate from my classes. A few became full-time Comedians. Others, full time Pastors.

Pat K.

One of my students was Pat. She was a wonderful young lady who weighted over 400 lbs.

During the workshop, she had to go on stage and tell jokes about her weight. In the beginning she wasn't comfortable, but I spent a lot of time with Pat after class talking about her problem. What she liked about her weight and what she hated about her weight. She ended up feeling comfortable joking about her weight, and the crowd loved it at the graduation party. Pat lost over 250 lbs. since taking the class.

Lance E.

Another student of mine was Lance. He was a Deacon at a church and a closet alcoholic. He didn't share that with many people, but while taking the class, and getting the confidence that he was funny, following graduation, he joined an AA meeting. He is now sober and Pastors a local church.

Ron M.

One time I was preparing for a class when my friend Annie told me about one of her employees, Ron, a Korean-Irish guy. I went to the store to meet him. He was hilarious. I asked him if he ever considered doing Comedy. He wasn't sure. I insisted that he take my Comedy Workshop. He did and I'm glad he did. I can tell you he is glad he did. He took two workshops and then started opening for me. We would drive to shows together. Ron, in my opinion, is one of the funniest guys to be around. His ad-libs _are_ amazing.

Even though he was a newer Comedian at the time, we still added him to our Comedy writing group. Ron is now a full-time Comedian as I write this book and has been for a while.

Taylor T.

One of the other people worth mentioning is Taylor Tomlinson. Taylor was one of the finalists on Last Comic Standing and now is the host of FOX Laughs. She came to my class at the age of 16 with her dad. He wanted to do something together with his daughter and brought her along. Taylor was shy but amazingly sarcastic. I knew right away that she has great potential in Comedy. She attended a second workshop and started opening for me. A year later, her dad sent her to Cal Poly University in

San Luis Obispo. I called her few months later and asked her to quit and come back to Southern California. I don't think her dad was very happy with that decision, but I knew that living in Central California would kill her Comedy Career. Taylor listened to me and moved back to Southern California and attended a local college. She focused on her career and applied what she learned from my classes. Soon, Taylor started doing the college circuit and started generating good money.

When she became a host on FOX Laughs, all the guilt I felt for asking someone's daughter to leave her education and pursue Comedy was gone. I don't feel guilty anymore but feel proud of Taylor.

Daniel J

One time I attended a Barnabas Group Meeting in the Inland Empire at the Teen Challenge. Teen Challenge is a place where young men in a drug rehabilitation program can go for further spiritual training, academic and vocational preparation before reentering society. The Barnabas group, on the other hand, is a gathering of marketplace leaders where they listen to the needs of various ministries and offer help to them. It is a greet meeting between the "haves" and the "wants".

While seated at the table, Margarete, one of the leaders, introduced me to Daniel J. He was a graduate of Teen Challenge. He is the son of a Pastor from San Diego. Daniel did Comedy here and there as an 18-year-old, then on the day he proposed to his wife, he was in a car accident and injured himself. He was heavily medicated and became addicted to pain medication. That led him to heroin. For few years, Daniel was addicted to heroin until he joined Teen Challenge in Riverside, CA.

Daniel mentioned once to Margarete that he wanted to be a Comedian and that some Comedian named Nazareth, was one of his idols (not sure why. He must've been high when he thought that!). Well, that night Daniel was sitting at my table (God's timing) and we got introduced. He seemed like a very nice and smart young man. He shared with me his desire to do Comedy. I told him that if he was serious about doing it, I could help him, but he must stay sober at all times.

I met with Daniel several times and helped him start his act. I've also had him open for me at Angel's Camp. He now works for me and opens for me regularly.

Teen Suicide

Speaking of Angel's Camp, I'm reminded of my friend Shawn M, with whom I developed a friendship many years ago. I spoke at a camp for Calvary Chapels Youth Pastors in Grass Valley, CA, and I was sharing a message to encourage Youth Pastors not to look for numbers and be impressed by churches who had a huge Youth Group, but to be faithful to the few young people God entrusted them with.

That caught the attention of my friend Shawn, and we clicked. He invited me to Northern California to speak at his events. I've been up there so many times that on one afternoon I was in Sonora and I entered a furniture store. They were playing my CD. I jokingly asked the cashier if she knew who was that funny Comedian they were playing? She replied, "I don't know his name, but he sounds like you!" Yes. I'm big in Sonora, CA.

Later, Shawn and his wife Connie, who both have hearts of gold and are on their third adoption, moved to Angel's Camp near Sonora, CA and took over a dying church.

They're thriving now.

A few years ago, Shawn, who also coached the High School football team for Angel's Camp, called me and sounded sad. I asked what happened, and he told me that another teenager committed suicide in that school. Calaveras County, according to the Calaveras Enterprise, has one of the State's highest suicide rates.

Shawn asked me to bring the "Laughter For All" Crusade to Angel's Camp to bring some hope. And hope we did bring to Angel's Camp. We filled up the High School theatre and at the end of the event, when I gave the invitation, 16 teens came forward to receive Christ.

That is the ultimate hope. We went back to Angel's Camp early this year and did another concert.

A Marine and a Middle Easterner

I arrived with Doc to Poulsbo. It was a beautiful outdoor stage overlooking the lake. A crowd of 1000 people were seated on the grass facing the stage. A band called Love and the Outcome were performing. I followed them. While I was sharing how proud I was to be an American, a Marine cut through security and walked up to the stage and hugged me and started crying. I was honestly scared in the beginning. I looked at his hands to see if he was carrying a gun or a knife.

Right before he came up to the stage, I was sharing a joke about how after 911, people were afraid to sit next to me on the plane. So, when he got to me and hugged me, he whispered in my ear, "I will fly next to you."

I felt at that moment that this Marine just wanted to hug a Middle Eastern person. It was more for his inner struggle. One of the two security personal guarding the stage looked at me and I gave him the OK nod. I kept hugging that young Marine and asked him few questions and then he was escorted away by the security to people's applause. Usually when my act is interrupted by a heckler, it can be upsetting. This time it was a privilege to get off track.

I love moments like these where my Comedy and my life can be healing to somebody.

And that's what this book is for.

CONCLUSION

My goal for this book was to show you, through stories and events that happened in my life, the proof that God's plans are often different than our plans. I want you to see and believe that tomorrow can bring a whole new solution that you never even thought about. You can wake up to events not on your Things-To-Do-Today list. Situations can arise that you didn't write about in your journal.

Faith

When I walked into that small Southern Baptist Church on a Sunday Morning in August 1992, I had no clue what was about to happen. I didn't have the slightest inkling that my entire life was about to be completely changed in that moment. My outlook on life, my idea of God, my faith, my belief system; they all changed in a heartbeat. All I could say was that I was blind, but now I could see.

I had Hope in 24 Hours.

Relationships

When I arrived in the Gaza Strip on that August day in 1995, I didn't know that my life was about to change again. On that day, I met the woman God had prepared for me. I was a miserable passenger on that flight from Amsterdam to Tel Aviv. I didn't want to leave the US, leave my shows and come to the Gaza Strip, but I did it for my dad. Had I known that on that day I would meet the love of my life, my best friend, my bride, I would've been dancing in the aisle on that plane (or at least wiggling a lot more in my seat).

But I didn't. It wasn't on my Things-To-Do-Today list or it wasn't one of my New Year Resolutions.

We met, and our lives changed. One day I was single, 24 hours later (after she said "yes") I was planning a wedding.

Hope in 24 Hours.

Finances

The third one is when my friend called me, asked how I was doing, and sent me a check for $100,000. That God did that still blows me away. The day before, I owed the bank late payments more than $70,000. The next day, I was up-to-date with my mortgage payment.

Hope in 24 Hours.

Life and Death

I will never forget Fadi's story of being released by ISIS and my own story of narrowly escaping the Café bombing, had I stayed there for just 10 more minutes.

Any of this could happen to you too before the end of today. Maybe by tomorrow. Perhaps a day or two after tomorrow. You don't know. Why then waste your life worrying about things you have no control over? The Bible commands us not to worry or be anxious about tomorrow.

Do you know why we worry about tomorrow? Because we assume several things:

1- Nothing will change

2- God is not in control

3- Life will go from bad to worse

I'm not suggesting that every problem you have will be solved, that every sickness will be healed, every debt will be paid, but what I am saying is that living with that pessimistic mentality that nothing will ever improve, is wrong, and will deteriorate your health.

I hope this book encouraged you to have hope; to trust God more and to be thankful for a great nation that offers us an environment for change for the better.

Would you please consider the very things that concern you? Things that you don't have a solution for; situations you're afraid of. Stop thinking of your own path to the solution and for a few minutes, just pray and ask God to solve it His way!

Timothy Keller, an American Pastor, best known as the founding Pastor of Redeemer Presbyterian Church in New York City, in one of his sermons on the Wisdom book of Proverbs, compares the fatalistic approach to life to the American approach to life.

He compares the fatalistic approach to life that states that your destiny is fixed, regardless of your choices. He says that there is the American approach that states that your choices will determine your future. That if you make good choices, you will have a good future and vice versa.

While I do agree that's partially true, there is also the Biblical approach that states that while your choices are your responsibility, your future is absolutely controlled by God.

My choices belong to me, but at the same time, my future is both designed and determined under the sovereignty of God. God can intervene in my life at any time, regardless of my choices and change my path.

If you have a story that relates to hope in 24 hours. Something that happened to you in one day that changed the course of your life, please go to our website *www.Hopein24hours.com* and share it with us. I trust it will encourage other readers.

Thank you for taking the time to read this book.

STORIES FROM
MY FRIENDS
THAT FOUND HOPE
IN 24 HOURS

Brian's Story:

It was February 11th, 2000, and my sister-in-law called me to tell me that I really ought to go to the hospital my father was in, because my mother was with him and she needed some comfort and to be relieved for a bit.

He had just been admitted a couple days prior because he had taken a turn for the worst. He had been diagnosed with lung cancer six weeks prior, which had metastasized to his brain. He was showing stroke-like symptoms, but once he got to the hospital on New Year's Eve 1999, he and my mom got the bad news. It didn't help that the doctor had very poor bedside manors. Mom was a career nurse. It's how she met my dad in the military in

Spokane, WA. My mom from eastern PA and my dad from east Texas were worlds away from where they grew up when they married. Now their relationship was at critical mass.

I had grown up Catholic. Nothing against them, because I did learn a lot of respect and honor in that stream of the faith. Confession, communion, serving as an altar boy and going on retreats with the other kids gave me a sense of community, but I found a way out of it from time to time. But I wandered far, and the Lord brought be back . . . hard!

I tried to evangelize my family, but they were offended that I thought they needed it. My mom sort of kept to herself, while my dad, who was raised Baptist, just told me he just wanted me to live it and not tell him about it. He once even put his hand almost in my face as I shared the love of God meant for him through Jesus Christ. He resisted for years.

I was going to a church that was moving in signs and wonders type of teaching, but I hadn't seen any of it when I was converted back in 1981. I went to a conference in1984 and decided to get prayer to bring this power stuff in to my life. It came fast, and I heard God way more clearly, and things started to take off. I had just graduated with a music degree when I saw others come to Christ around me. I wasn't doing too many gigs, like I really wanted to as a musician, so I went to the music store one year and picked up a guitar with my tax return. I began to lead worship, and with that came the responsibility, like other leadership roles in the church, to seek the Lord for wisdom in leading His people.

I began hearing His voice more and more, and at one point, I heard He could speak in visions and dreams. This was interesting to me, since I'm the more creative, left-brained kind of person.

Well, it happened in 1983 or '84. I sat there seeking the Lord in prayer, like I was prone to do just about daily, and He revealed something to me. I didn't like it.

What I saw was my dad in a hospital bed in the far end of a double occupancy hospital room, with the other bed empty. He was old and decrepit and not moving, hardly breathing. I saw the institutional pale green paint, the TV mounted to the ceiling to the left, he was to the right, near the window. Through the window, I saw the gray, overcast sky, and nobody was in the room. It was quiet. Too quiet. I then heard the Lord speak softly that He would use me to usher my dad in to His presence, on his deathbed.

I immediately said 'No, Lord'! How's that for a complete sentence? Totally incongruous.

A complete oxymoron. 'I want him to enjoy you for the rest of his life.' That went over like a lead balloon. No matter what I said or prayed, it seemed like nothing would change that vision.

That vision appeared to me about 40-50 times over the course of about 17-18 years, until I would just think, 'oh, that THING again', or, 'oh, no, not that again.' I got used to it. If I was day dreaming a little, or maybe a little tired, it would pop right before my eyes, more real than the things in the room right in front of me.

I told a few people, and when I had become engaged and gotten married, it was one of those things that I told my wife. I gave her the details, the green institutional paint, gray skies through the window, empty bed next to my dad and the TV, all with him old and shriveled and ready to die.

Fast forward to the day my sister-in-law called. I was at work and was headed home. I called my wife and told her I was going to the hospital to be with my mom and dad. I asked her, 'do you remember the vision I told you that I had 40-50 times about my dad?' She said 'yes'. I said, 'well, I think that this is that'. She was leaving the house, but I asked her to put out a sandwich and a Bible for me, so I could run in to the house, pick them up, and bolt straight to the hospital.

When I got there, I rushed up to the 3rd floor where my dad was. I made my way down the hall looking for his room. I went past a few rooms, but I kept looking for my dad's. I went past the nurses' station, and his room was on the left. I entered slowly, and I was awe-struck, amazed, and terrified. Here it was. The pale institutional green painted room, TV on the ceiling to the left, dad to the right, near the window, with the gray overcast skies outside, next to him, and empty bed. My mom was there, and gave me a hug, told me to get him a drink if he needed it, and that she'd go home and get a bit to eat and check her answering machine, make a few calls and come back to relieve me. She left, and I was left there sitting on a chair, right next to my sleeping, very sick father.

I prayed in my mind, 'Lord, now it's ALL on You. I don't know what to do, nothing else has worked, and You need to do something. I can't do a thing'. Just at that very moment, a friend of my parents, who was a retired Catholic priest, walked through the door. I didn't know who he was but had heard about him. He approached the bed, my dad said hello to him, and introduced Father Di to me. (pronounced Dee from his last name DiPasquale).

Hmm, I thought to myself, 'this just got really interesting'. Father Di and I exchanged some small talk, then he turned his attention to my dad. 'Walt, would you like to pray?' he asked. 'Sure', said my dad. That was a surprise. I guess it's true that there are no fox hole atheists, or agnostics, or even backsliders.

Father Di and I grabbed my dad's hands, one from each side of the bed.

Side note: we evangelicals have this lingo we use about getting 'saved' or 'accepting the Lord'. You know. Heads bowed, eyes closed, raise your hand, walk to the front, pray the 'Sinners Prayer' with the guy up front. Interesting. It's not in the Bible. None of this 'you gotta do stuff' mentality is in the Bible about trusting in Christ. It says to believe He died for you and was raised from the dead. That's it.

Father Di began to pray the most beautiful prayer I think I ever heard in my life. Such revelation. Such simplicity. Such an answer to MY prayer. He said:

> 'Father, YOU be Walt's strength.
>
> Jesus, YOU be Walt's salvation.
>
> Holy Spirit, YOU be Walt's comfort.'

He may have prayed some more than that, but I was in such tearful shambles as soon as he began praying, that I didn't know what else he prayed. It was beautiful, but such audacity to actually put the responsibility of my dad's salvation on God's shoulders?

Hmm . . . .

Just as Father Di finished, I heard my dad sigh. It was a fairly big exhale, being that his lung capacity in his sickness had been greatly reduced.

He looked at me with his beautiful blue eyes and winked. 'I'm gonna' be ok,' he said to me. I was doing my best to wipe my eyes and nose with a sleeve or two as he stared up to me. You don't want to be crying at a dying person's bedside, now do you?

But I had just witnessed a miracle. A fulfillment of a vision, the salvation of my dad, and I didn't have to do a thing except wrestle with a vision enough to pray for my dad for a few years. That was nothing compared to now knowing that I would see him in heaven.

I learned that it wasn't about my witnessing ability, which admittedly, isn't the best. It wasn't about how much I could tell him about the Bible. It had nothing to do with me and my 'just do it' attitude and lifestyle. There's nothing I could have done to speed up the outcome, except pray, live the life Jesus wanted me to live, and to accept the love He had for me. That's how we operate. That's our fuel. That's what it takes to go through this life and its ups and downs, is to lean heavily on God, and take everything He has to offer to us. We can only do ministry if we 'leak' who God really is, through us. We can't work it, display it, manufacture it, pretend it, organize it, build it, or DO it any other way. HE has to. And He wants to do it THROUGH us.

Now, is it a big deal that a priest came in to a hospital room of a dying friend and prayed with the man and his son? Not really. I'm sure it happens often. That priest came in to a room of a PRAYING son, who was torn about his dad, and had a Buddhist brother and two unconverted brothers who were not having visions about the man who was dying.

God knew at all times He could save my dad. Could He have wanted to show ME that He doesn't work in ways I think He should? Was He trying to tell me that He loved me, even in my father's dire circumstance? Was He in this? I think so.

Father Di shook my hand and left. My mom came in a few minutes later and I told her Father Di was just there. I was still in shock.

I told my dad I loved him and that I'd see him tomorrow. He said, 'I love you too.' They were his last words to me. Just then, the news was on in his room, showing a space shuttle Endeavor launch that happened that day. Just whose endeavor was my dad's salvation?

The next morning, I was called to come to the hospital. My dad was unresponsive and had slipped in to a coma. His pulse was getting weaker and the nurses told us that it wouldn't be long. Father Di popped his head in to the room and came in and prayed with the whole family. He told us to encircle dad's bed, join hands, and tell him it was ok to go. Dad's breathing weakened, and slowly stopped while I was right next to him.

Boy, was that hard. But it was easier for me than for anyone else in the room. I knew where he was going, and that I'd see him soon.

I was crying about my dad's death, so was everyone else. But I had a different experience. I saw God come through this vision and build my faith 1,000,000%! My faith was like the Grinch's heart. It grew. In one day. 24 hours. From near death, to eternal life, to bodily death. My dad was transformed.

Alisa G: A Christmas Angel...In Red Plaid

"Hot, dry Santa Ana winds are expected until Christmas Day," the radio host announced on a particularly warm California day in 1992.

"You be careful driving down the mountain," my husband said to me. "Watch out for rocks on the road."

My heart sank. A dangerous drive was not on my shopping list. Before leaving, I gave our one-year-old daughter a cuddle and hugged our three-year-old son.

My husband and I were struggling financially, and just two days before Christmas my parents had called and said that they were coming up to spend the night Christmas Eve so that they could be there in the morning when the children opened their presents.

This was the very first time my parents had ever offered to spend the night and I was so excited that they were coming up the mountain to visit! I wanted everything to be perfect for them. We decided to give them our bedroom and we'd sleep in the twin beds in our son's room. But . . . our mattress was worn, saggy, and in terrible shape, and we needed another . . . right away.

I was on a mission to find a used mattress. Convinced that God gives us enough, the $50 in my purse just had to be sufficient for the task.

After my forty-five-minute drive, the very kind manager at a used furniture store bent over backwards and offered me an older king-sized mattress that looked nearly brand new, discounted from $200 down to $50. *Thank you, Lord*, I whispered in relief, tears pricking at the corners of my eyes. I knew that the manager was being incredibly gracious to a frantic young mom.

Two burly employees helped carry it out and hoist it onto the smooth dark blue roof of my tiny Dodge Colt hatchback, and that's when everyone realized we had a problem. The mattress hung down almost to the back bumper, drooping forward over the windshield about two feet, and over the doors by nearly two feet on each side.

The manager didn't think it was a good idea. "Don't you have someone with a truck who can come and pick it up?" he asked dubiously.

I shook my head, tears threatening. We'd only lived in Lake Arrowhead for a year, and I hadn't met many people there yet. "I've just got to make this work," I said, choking back my panic.

The employees brought out yards of wide cotton strapping and it took a few minutes to realize that I had to roll down all four windows, get into the car, and close the driver's door before they could secure the load. Then the workers wound the straps across the mattress, over and over and over and through the windows, essentially tying all four doors shut. As I'm 6'1" tall, it was going to be a rather tight squeeze for me to crawl out the window once I got home, but I figured it was doable.

As I started to drive, the mattress immediately shifted and began to slip backwards off the roof. The men shouted at me to return. Next, they used additional strapping and lashed it to the front and rear bumpers as well. This seemed to work, but it had the effect of pushing the top of the mattress down over the windshield. Inside, the multiple lines of the white cording obscured some of my vision. I was putting myself at risk over a mattress . . . and I knew it was foolish, but I stubbornly chose to continue.

The drive from the store to home was 27 miles—and on a good day, it took about 40 minutes on the highway. Today, I figured it'd take a bit longer on the surface streets. As I started out one more time, it was with great relief. The mattress was holding firm and steady, despite the strong winds blowing. When I accelerated to 20 miles per hour, I could feel the mattress begin to tug and lift a bit, straining at the straps. My heart leapt into my throat, and I tried to keep my nerves under control. I slowed down to 15 miles per hour and the movement diminished. Nevertheless, I spent a lot of time praying as I drove, "Lord, help me get there safely."

All went well until I began to climb up the mountain. There, the Santa Ana winds were gusting and blowing with greater force, buffeting my car back and forth. I slowed down to a crawl. There was no way to turn around—I would have to continue.

On the way, I prayed for traveling mercies and sang praises

to keep the ever-rising tide of panic from taking over. I shrieked occasionally when particularly hard gusts blew down the pass, and I feared they would tip over my compact Colt. While I crept forward, commuters rushed past me and honked, horns blaring their anger and irritation at the stupidity of someone bringing a mattress up on such an evening, but I was at least making progress.

As I rounded a broad, wide turn, the change in position put me head-on into the worst yet of the Santa Ana blasts. In that moment, the mattress lifted clear off the roof, straining wildly against the strapping. It made a twanging sound much like a banjo string being plucked. The little Dodge was too light, the mattress too large, and the winds too strong; the vehicle lifted entirely off the ground and literally flew backwards for a foot or two before slamming down on all four wheels with a bounce and a thud.

"Oh, Lord, help me!" I cried in terror. After the tires hit the ground, I braked as hard as I could—as if that would keep the car from going airborne again. After a few moments, I began creeping forward foot by foot, fighting the gusts, and feeling them rocking and lifting and shoving against the car.

The ridiculousness of the situation struck me, and I laughed in spite of the dread and anxiety. I had a vision of Sally Fields in the Flying Nun being lifted by her wimple, but instead I was driving a flying mattress car.

Then, as I was passing the largest turnout on the mountain highway, another enormous blast of wind slammed into the car.

My heart froze as the mattress sprang out like an umbrella, lifting over two feet from the roof of the car, restrained only by the cotton wrapping, which stretched and bowed from the incredible force of the Santa Ana's. The Dodge Colt rose off the ground once more and sailed many feet to the right—across the wide turnout and directly toward a thousand-foot cliff. Hanging onto the wheel and braking for no rational reason, I screamed out to God, "Save me! Lord, save me!"

The car jolted down once, jarring my teeth from the force, lifted up again, and sailed another ten feet—and then crashed into twin wooden power line poles, just a few feet from the edge of the cliff. Three feet forward or backward, and I would have gone over the edge.

Because the car had been blowing sideways and because it was several feet in the air when it hit the poles, the vehicle landed at a 45-degree angle, wedged tightly. I tried to climb out, but the car threatened to overturn, and I did not wish to crush my arms or body, so I gingerly eased back into the driver's seat, trembling.

By now, darkness was falling. The hot, dry Santa Ana winds turned frigid as daylight drained into dusk. My headlights pointed off the edge of the turnout, the curve of the road hiding me from any passing traffic. Cell phones didn't exist yet—at least—not for people who didn't have a great deal of money. The chill air only made me feel more alone, cold, and frightened. Nearly out of gasoline, I turned off the car's engine.

Ant-trails of lights from other cars coming and going up and down Highway 18 marked the road, but none seemed able to see me, even when I flashed my lights continuously. After thirty minutes, it was full-dark, and my headlights grew dim. The old battery couldn't hold out, so I shut them off and prayed.

"Lord, I need some rescuing here ... please send me an angel!"

Seconds after uttering my heartfelt prayer, two beams illumi-nated the turnout. I worried my car would be mistaken for just an old abandoned mattress up against the poles. The glow of the headlights came straight on, and soon a large pick-up truck rolled up alongside my little car.

I breathed a sigh of relief. Help was here. A HUGE man got out of the truck, and I gulped, my relief evaporating at the sight. He looked like a lumberjack, dressed in a red plaid flannel shirt and dark blue jeans, and his broad shoulders and his height made my tall family seem petite. "Ma'am, you look like you've got yourself in spot of trouble," he said in a thick southern accent.

At that, he reached into a sheath attached to his belt and drew out an enormous knife.

I'm going to be murdered, I panicked. *No, no, no! My babies! My family!*

The burly young man slashed through the strapping with ease. I flinched away when he put both of his hands through the driver's side window and *lifted* the entire car and placed it back onto all four wheels. Without speaking another word, he hoisted the mattress, carried it over to his truck and gently placed it down. That mattress fit perfectly in the bed of his Ford.

He came over and laid what seemed like a healing hand on the hood of my battered car, leaned in and said in that Southern drawl, "I believe that your car should be able to drive now. Follow me, I'll take you home."

Despite the battery wearing down, the impact of the crash, and the weight of the mattress on a car that had been balancing on two wheels, my car sprang to life and drove as well as it ever had. The blowing winds were not as significant with the mattress off my car, and my internal shaking began to subside as I followed the Ford pick-up the rest of the way up the mountain. On the way, I had plenty of time to recognize that I had not told the man where I lived, nor had I ever seen him before, nor did I even know his name. We got to my home without incident and he lifted the mattress effortlessly, carried it down the flight of stairs to the entrance of our home, and placed it against the wall. He nodded at me and said warmly, "I hope you have a Merry Christmas."

"Thank you so, so much!!!" I said with gratitude and a heart filled to overflowing with praise. I blurted out awkwardly, "What's your name? Would you like to come in for some hot chocolate?"

"It's time for me to go," he smiled at me, and as he walked away he said, "May God bless you today and always."

Multiple emotions crashed about me as I tried to fully comprehend what had just happened. That Christmas, and every Christmas after, has been even more meaningful, for now I know, without any doubt, that God had sent me an angel.

Kellie B: The Truck

I was in dark place in my life! I had accepted the Lord years prior but didn't really understand the true meaning behind it. I grew up Catholic. But anyway, my journey in life was definitely not what God had in mind for me. I was on a very self-destructive path.

One morning on my way to a meeting my truck broke down and I decided to step in front of my truck to see if I could fix the problem. That was the last thing I remember. A lady had impacted the rear of my truck in which my truck impacted me. It was a life changing moment! God was not ready for me yet. It not only changed where my life was at that time, but it brought me home.

Later my mother was diagnosed with stage 4 colon cancer. I got to spend 8 years with her. The best gift that I was able to give my mother was that she was able to see me turn my life around and go to college and earn my bachelor's degree before she passed away. Looking back, it made me realize that even in the bad God brings good into it. I thank God for his intervention and the blessings He has shown me!

Deann A: The Bullet sent from Heaven.

Just thought I share a bit of a life changing moment! I spent most of my teen years and much of my adult life trying to save Mama from herself. Since her first psychotic episode in the late 1950s until her death in 2010, she underwent no fewer than 20 psychiatric hospitalizations. I remember as a 15-year-old having to trick her into going to the hospital, conniving ways to keep her locked in the house when she wasn't taking her meds, running interference between her and those disrupted by her behavior, including her employers.

We lived in the 'hood on DuPont Street in Shreveport, Louisiana, 71103, listed as the poorest zip code in the state. A crack house was across the street. In the late 1980s the grandma who lived two blocks away and planned activities for the neighborhood nursing home was stopped at a red light a quarter-mile from Mama's house when somebody trying to steal her car shot her. Whoever was in the car with Miss Sarah tried to drive her to the hospital, but she bled to death en route.

Mama often refused to take her antipsychotic medicine. When she didn't take it, she hallucinated, heard voices, felt compelled to roam at night in her bedclothes. On DuPont Street, that's an invitation for a bullet in the head. At least twice a month a notice would arrive in Mama's mailbox that a criminal who lived nearby was about to be released from prison for sex crimes.

But as psychotic and gravely disabled as she was, Mama refused to leave DuPont Street. Her daddy had bought that house, she said. Though the family who held the title to a house across the street offered to sell it to Mama's neighbor Miss Mattie for $2000, Mattie turned down the offer. Likewise, Mama's house wasn't worth much, but it was all she owned in this world.

In 1999 after four months of psychiatric hospital treatment for yet another bout with refusing to self-medicate, her behavior remained unchanged. I lost a court case to have her declared mentally incompetent and forcibly committed to a place that would keep her safe.

As people around the world were praying for her, her illness worsened. After the doctor at last released her from outpatient care, she still refused to leave DuPont Street.

Because I lost the competency hearing, I couldn't force her to go anywhere. I went back home to Texas, waiting for the next phone call from friends, neighbors or loved ones demanding that I drop everything and run to Shreveport and "fix Martha."

A week later after that hospital discharge, she heard a big noise at 2:30 a.m. Sunday. When daylight came, she found a bullet hole in her bedroom wall, less than two feet from her head.

That Monday morning, not only did Mama voluntarily put her name on every senior citizen apartment waiting list in Shreveport, she was suddenly in her right mind. The bullet episode—a drive-by shooting targeting her next-door neighbor—triggered a "shock reflex'" in her brain that literally shocked her back to sanity.

When there was no way to force her from that dangerous neighborhood, the Lord answered our desperate prayers with a ricocheted bullet.

Bruce K: The Mission House

Bruce and Denise were in the process of building a Mission House on their property for Missionaries to stay when they were itinerating. It was on a Saturday that they were discussing that they were short $1000 that they needed for their mortgage on Monday. They had invested all their extra cash and credit cards and were pretty much maxed out because of the Mission House.

They got a call on Sunday from a couple that they had done some premarital counseling with just a couple years before who wanted to come over and see them. They were tired but they wanted to make room for ministering to this couple, but the couple would not tell them why they wanted to come over. The couple lived about 45 minutes away. They were pretty much newlyweds. So, Bruce and Denise were tired on that Sunday afternoon but said yes, they could come over.

When they showed up they were talking pretty much small talk and never really got to anything that seemed really important. But they said we really felt like we had to come over today. And after they finished small talk they pulled out a check that was already written and put it on the counter. They said goodbye and that was all. Bruce and Denise thought this young couple were really nice to do that, but they didn't think that it would be very much.

So, when the couple left Bruce picked up the check and looked at it and then looked at Denise and said you have to look at this check. She did not expect much. But when she looked at the check she began to cry, and he began to cry. The check was $1000.

The young couple Brian and Brenda had no idea that Bruce

and Denise were really strapped for funds. But their obedience to the Lord in their sensitivity to his voice changed the situation so that Bruce and Denise could continue building the Mission House.

God is seldom early but he's never late. Since that time, the Mission House after it was finished has hosted over 900+ Missionaries and Ministers rent free.

Michelle H: Cancer Gone

7 years ago, I was told I had breast cancer. The "good kind," as if there's any such thing. I was obviously confused, mad, upset, afraid to tell my family, you name it I was afraid of it. From the day the doctor told me this, I was on the operating table 10 days later.

My surgery was on a Monday. That weekend prior, I went to Palm Springs by myself and to climb Mount San Jacinto. My father had died 10 years prior and going through this diagnosis, made me miss him all the more. My father and I used to climb Mount San Jacinto every single year and I decided to go do that by myself and feel a little closer to him.

I got on the trail and started to climb, crying the entire way. Begging God to not leave my son an orphan. Begging God to give me peace. Begging God to let me be OK. About 1 mile from the peak, I had an overwhelming sense that somebody was with me. To the point that I was even looking around wondering if somebody had caught up to me. I was embarrassed to be crying. But there was nobody there.

In my mind and of course not audibly, I literally heard my father's voice say, "Everything will be OK." I could've sworn I felt his arm around my shoulders. And he repeated again "everything will be OK." It was the strangest thing that has ever happened to me, but in that moment, I knew everything was going to be OK. I had PEACE, I had hope, and I had more strength.

The next day I checked in at the hospital, signed all the necessary papers for the doctor to do what they had to do during surgery, not knowing what was going to happen when I woke up. When I woke up the doctor came to see me immediately and told me they got it all and that I was going to be just fine! Did not even have to have chemo. The funny thing is, I knew that before I was even put to sleep on the table.

So, I'm not sure if that something you're looking for, and obviously I can elaborate on details as that day of the climb is etched in my mind. And I don't tell many people the story, because they look at me strange but in that moment, I knew for a fact that the Lord was with me and he made everything OK.

Ray P:

If you were to draw a line in the sand, just as Jesus did, that's exactly how I picture my life in recovery. There was the old me and everything after that June 30th is the new me. I remember the events leading to that definitive moment in my life. I spent the night before binge drinking, drunk driving and barhopping with so-called "friends". I started the festivities early, what started as a celebratory drink turned into a whole day affair, eventually ending with myself passed out at work, only to be woken up by a group of 3 police cars shining their light into my office and tapping on my windows to do a wellness check, because I hadn't checked in for days and my wife and parents were worried for my erratic behavior.

Being an alcoholic, in my mind, at that very moment, I thought I was 6'5" and continued to mouth off and disrespect the officers. It wasn't until they threatened to arrest me for my conduct, did I finally smarten up and simmer down. It was a chaotic scene, which mirrored the turmoil in my personal and professional life.

I spent the night before my last drink in my old bedroom at my parent's home, because I had nowhere to go. I was separated from my wife and kicked out of my home. I remember lying there feeling sorry for myself, wondering where it all went wrong for me. Just a few years prior, I was being recognized in my career as an up and coming lawyer, making decent money, had the nice house, cars, private club memberships and every other superficial thing you could ask for.

However, on that particular night I lay in bed defeated; morally, spiritually and financially broke. I spent the 2 and ½ years leading up to that point drinking daily to numb myself of the work pressures and financial stress. When the real estate market and economy started to turn for the worse, we weren't affected at first. However, a little after a year later, I started to feel the pinch both at home and at work. Instead of making sound decisions, I took personal and business lines of credit to keep the business and my lifestyle afloat. Everything at that point had become a façade. I was leveraged with debt; this coupled with my drinking created the perfect storm. Eventually when the lines of credit froze, I dipped into my personal savings; thinking the entire time that everything could turn around any minute.

My wife, desperate to find help and support, had started coming to Crossroads Church regularly. We had been before but were very sporadic; still not willing to completely turn our lives over to the care of God. She started going to Al-Anon and soon after that, I found my way to Celebrate Recovery and joined my first 12 step study. Things looked promising, but a mere 30 days later I relapsed. Despite still drinking, I continued going to meetings, basically faking my way through them. My rock bottom kept getting deeper and deeper, eventually leading to the early morning of June 30th, with the police tapping on my window.

Later that day, my wife, Amy, showed up to my office and blocked my car in so I could not leave. I agreed to get in her car, where she drove me home and held an intervention. I was hesitant at first, but after talking to the counselor, my defenses slowly retreated. When we didn't have the money to pay for rehab, we found out that my wife's work unilaterally changed their benefits provider effective July 1st (it was a mandatory change in the health insurance) and that new insurance company DID pay for rehab. I entered treatment that same afternoon. God was at work in my life. After finding out that rehab would be 100% covered under the new insurance plan, I remember thinking "For all of these stars to align . . . for the new health insurance, which went into effect the next day, to fully pay for treatment, God must be really fighting for me."

Thankfully we serve a faithful and forgiving God. In the book of Isaiah, the Bible says that God, <u>no matter how deep the stain of our sins, will make us pure and white as snow</u>. Not only does he forgive us and give us a fresh start, the Bible says in the book of Hebrews, chapter 8, verse 12 that <u>God is so merciful that chooses not to remember our sins anymore</u>. Our slate is wiped completely clean.

So, if you are here tonight struggling or feeling guilty for your past, you can stop feeling sorry for yourself; you no longer need to be bound by the chains of your past. Rest assured, that God loves you so much that he sent his only son, Jesus, to die for your sins and make you white as snow. God has already forgiven you and wants to welcome you into His family with open arms.

The fact that I am before you tonight, clean and sober, living a transparent life, is a testament to the truth of God's love and forgiveness. No matter how far down you are, Jesus is in the business of miracles. Just as He did for me, He can save you from your situation and turn it into good for His kingdom and His purpose.

Jill B.

Tim and I had tried for 5 years to have children. We had been through every type of infertility treatment possible. And we were planning on spending quite a bit of money for IVF treatment. It was a difficult and sad time to find out I wasn't pregnant month after month.

I will never forget on one Sunday morning Tim and I attended service at Crossroads. This was when Pastor Barry M. was our Pastor at Crossroads. At the end of the service he had everyone hold hands and he announced he would like to make a special prayer to all the couples who are experiencing infertility in their lives.

There were probably a good 300 people at the service that day. He looked directly at me while he said these words.

I, of course, went into the ugly cry and had no tissues and was holding a stranger's hand to the left of me. I'm sure that stranger thought I lost my mind. Haha!

Well, 3 months later a miracle happened. I was pregnant with Riley! I was getting to the point where I thought it would never happen and it did! After 5 years!

I was blessed with a miracle that day! I will never forget it as long as I live!

OTHER PRODUCTS
OFFERED BY NAZARETH:

COMEDY:

Free To Laugh DVD
Main Feature 49 min. + Bonus Feature 29 min.
@2007 By Horizon Media

Sweet Laughter DVD
Side-Splitting Laughter & Encouragement with Award Winning Comedian, Nazareth.
Bonus Features include: New up and coming Comedienne, Taylor Tomlinson 2013/Color/Run time: 85 min

Laugh Your Fears Away DVD
By Award Winning Comedian, Nazareth.

BOOKS:

You're So Funny Daddy –

Learning How To Communicate With Your Children Using Humor. You're So Funny, Daddy! speaks directly to Fathers who want to be Dads, But the ideas, concepts and thoughts shared in these pages are also a tremendous help to Mothers, Grandparents, Teachers, and any Father figure.

This book will help you communicate better with your children, and this will lead to a more rewarding relationship and happiness at home.

TEACHING:

On The Road to Eternity – 5 CD's Audio Teaching

Five Sermons, taped at various churches around the Country, which will sure encourage you.

To order these products go to: *www.NazarethUSA.com* or contact Comedy Crusade at 1-877-266-3392 to speak to a live person.